Nobody's Rag Doll

I0103331

Kate Swift

chipmunkapublishing
the mental health publisher

Kate Swift

Published by
Chipmunkapublishing
PO Box 6872
Brentwood
Essex CM13 1ZT
United Kingdom

http://www.chipmunkapublishing.com

Copyright © Kate Swift 2011

Edited by Katrina Bourke

ISBN 978-1-84991-643-1

Chipmunkapublishing gratefully acknowledge the support of Arts Council England.

Foreword

Following the success of her first book, 'This Tangled Web', Kate had many requests for more detail about her life and experiences to date, and the result is Nobody's Rag Doll. I am delighted to have the opportunity once again to write an introductory contribution from a professional viewpoint. What is striking as you travel her Journey through the book is the incredible resilience that Kate has demonstrated to survive such emotional extremes.

She has clearly articulated the damage caused when growing up in such a dysfunctional family where her needs were not even known, let alone met. It is a common feature of such families that they get trapped in a cycle of repetitive crises and problems, and trying the same approach to solving them that invariably fails. What happens is that the solution becomes the problem. No matter how many times they apply the same old solution the outcome will be the same; nothing fundamentally changes. Her family have continued to use an avoidant coping strategy; that is, keep ignoring the elephant in the room even though they all keep bumping into it! Growing up in such a stuck, unstable, unsafe and emotionally volatile environment, Kate is left with no option but to try and get her needs met elsewhere.

Her relationship with Molly is a good example of how Kate did manage to find for herself somewhere so emotionally nourishing, safe and stable that she would habitually spend hours there to soak up what she was denied at home. It is evident that Kate's own mother and father had serious problems of their own, but this does not allow them to abdicate responsibility for their parenting failures throughout Kate's life. Her mother's response to the sexual abuse disclosure and later Kate's attempted suicide are just two examples of her mother having no idea about her needs, and being more concerned about her own.

Throughout the book one cannot but admire the fact that Kate has survived so many difficult episodes in her life. Through the work she has done herself and with some professional input, she has managed to develop a very mature appropriate understanding of her experiences. It is especially pleasing to see how Kate has now been able to channel her energies from this understanding into promoting a greater public awareness of childhood sexual abuse from a survivor's viewpoint, and help victims via her Facebook group.
I am sure that all who read this book will find it heart-warming and informative, and have a deeper understanding of Kate the survivor.

Christopher Moore MSc
Schema Therapist (ISST)
Cognitive-behavioural Psychotherapist (BABCP)

Why tell my story?

In recent months since the release of my first book 'This Tangled Web', many survivors have asked me if my first book is my story; in a sense it is, through the form of poetry. The more people asked me the more I came to realise to my surprise that people actually wanted to hear and to read my own story. My closest friend Sophie has said many times about me writing a more autobiographical account of my life but I always used to laugh it off. It never occurred to me that I would have anything that interesting to say in this format. But I decided to sit down at the computer one day and just see if I could actually tell my story in this very direct and personal way. The first few lines came to me and I had them buzzing around inside me head for a few days. I felt the need to write them down and so it went from there and became the book you have in your hands today.

People need to be aware of the good that our system does and, equally so, its failings. They need to hear the survivor's voice, how they think and feel about how they are treated by the system. We cannot effect change if we are not made aware of what is happening within our social services departments, our hospitals and all the other public sectors working with people who have been abused. When I built my website (www.thistangledweb.co.uk) in February 2010 I was anxious to hear about a change within the way survivors are treated. Sometimes our public sector does a fantastic job but other times it falls down, and when it falls down a person – a child – is on the receiving end of those failures. In this book you will hear both good and bad.

The events detailed in this book are as I remember them to be. They are recorded as accurately as my memory will serve me. Some of the names, however, are fictional names.

I remember my own thirst for other people's stories and for information on childhood abuse when I first told of what had happened to me. I needed something to relate to, something to let me know that what I was feeling was 'normal', but most of all I needed someone to give me some hope when I was fresh out of my own. The books I read were a very important part of my early attempts to make some sense of, and begin to recover from, what had happened to me as a child. I have tried to carry this with me as I have written my own story, trying not to hold back and trying to be as honest as I possibly can be. That is what I believe will be most helpful to other survivors who read my story. If this book can play a part in another survivor's recovery then I feel like writing this book will have been more than worthwhile.

Please note that whilst I have made many references to what has helped me on my own healing journey through this wilderness, I am not a trained professional and these are simply my own tried and tested ways of what has helped me through. I would always recommend that you seek professional help and advice alongside anything you read. Further sources of help and information are listed towards the end of this book. One thing I have learnt for certain is that as survivors we are no longer alone and there are some excellent organisations/charities and individuals working to build a bridge from being a victim to a survivor.

~

Kate Swift

This book is dedicated to Molly…

This book is dedicated to the memory of my dear friend Molly who I love with all my heart. Molly had to triumph over adversity many times in her life; she was a people person with a heart of liquid gold. Molly kept me going with her warm smile, a squeeze of the hand, tea and, most importantly of all, hugs. Molly, you will never be forgotten.

Kate Swift

Acknowledgements

I want to thank my foster family – I will never forget the kindness that you showed me – for giving me a home and for sparing me from being placed into the care of complete strangers.

I want to thank Chipmunka Publishing for giving me a platform on which to be heard.

My thanks to David and the church for your love, care and support. Especially Jane for helping me to chase the rainbows and walking with me through some of the hardest parts of my recovery.

My thanks to Sophie and her family.

Sophie, thank you for your loving friendship and for encouraging me to write this book, and helping me to believe that I could write it and that people would want to read what I have to say.

I want to also acknowledge all the amazing survivors I am meeting along this journey. You truly are inspirational and courageous men and women. My thanks to all who encourage and support what I endeavour to do to make a difference for others.

Kate Swift

I was aware of the milkman outside on our street, that familiar humming of the milk float and the clinking of the bottles. It was a sunny day outside, one of those perfect summer mornings full of promise. Inside it was another regular day in our house. The washing machine was whirring in the kitchen and mum was back and forth pegging out the washing. I was in the sitting room curled up on the sofa watching cartoons on the television. Oh, the bliss of those long holidays from school. However, this particular summer was just about to bring the darkest storm cloud into my eight-year-old existence and change my life forever.

I was born in the spring of 1977, the youngest of six children. I was born with a hole in my heart and in need of what was then considered quite major heart surgery. Now it is done with a keyhole procedure. I am told that is why my parents have no baby photographs of me…should anything have happened to me they didn't want reminders. I find this rather odd as for me I am certain I would feel the opposite way round. I would want to cherish every moment I had with my baby girl. So it is that I have no photographs of me as a baby and just a handful of me growing up. In my earliest photo I guess I am approximately four to five years old. I still smile when I see the photo of me and my bike…a red bike (my favourite colour), with a carousel sticker and stabilisers. I don't have lots of memories of my early years, just a few significant moments that remain. I can very clearly remember my first day at school; I remember mum taking me into the classroom and sitting me down next to a neighbour's little girl. Mum placed a tissue up my sleeve and asked the girl next to me to look after me. I loved Primary school; it was my safe and happy world.

Life was pretty 'normal' back then, I guess. I idolised my mother right from when I was a very small child. We lived in a three bedroom council house on a quiet estate; I liked the little estate where I grew up and I still like the familiarity of some of the characters, who have lived in the street for as long as I can remember. Our street was a very friendly one; my parents had lived there a long time. People didn't tend to come and go where we lived and so you knew the people living in your street. Our school was just a very short walk away from home and we had several parks close by. We had a girls bedroom in the middle and then my parents' bedroom on one side and the boys' bedroom the other side. We were fortunate to have a large back garden, which was the setting for many a childhood pastime...playing camps, obstacle courses, hopscotch, making mud pies and various other games. I have lots of happy memories of playing in the garden; mostly I was happiest playing on my own. Playing my make-believe games of 'mums & dads' and creating a perfect scene where everyone was happy and everything was just right.

Our house was full of pets; other children used to visit and go home saying they had been to the zoo. At one point we had a dog, a hamster, a rabbit, a terrapin, a guinea pig, goldfish, budgies and other birds. At primary school in the juniors my best friend Sophie and I were up for saving the animals! We were very interested in charities such as the WWF and we made our own little newsletter about the plight of some of the endangered species. Even then I was trying to rescue and save but I could not rescue the things closest to my heart.

My sister and I have always had a love/hate relationship. We had the most furious arguments as children. When I think about our behaviour now I feel it was extreme even for sibling rivalry. After one argument my sister destroyed my bed; I mean, literally breaking it up so that I could not sleep in it. Another time she threw all my toys out of the upstairs bedroom window to the garden below. I once retaliated and broke her doll's face; I feel badly about that even now! I had a pet gold fish which my sister killed deliberately out of spite. She put washing up liquid into the water. I know it was a long time ago and some would say it was only a goldfish, but, even so, it was 'my' goldfish. We found few common bonds growing up, but one we did share was collecting stickers! Every Saturday we would walk to the local shop to spend our pocket money on packets of stickers, and then we would swap the doubles. We also liked looking through the catalogues and choosing what we would have in our own house, which was fun. There was a lot of jealousy with me being the youngest. I know as a teenager my sister was troubled but I don't know for certain the reasons behind it. Although we had, even as children, those divided loyalties, mine was always to mum and hers was to dad.

My parents met at senior school and so I always assumed it was a 'first love' thing. However, mum said she got married dressed all in black as that was how she felt on her wedding day. Apparently it was a day of thick fog and the registrar almost didn't make it into work to marry them. My father was quite a distant and cold figure. He owned a successful business but he also drank the profits away very successfully too. I guess that is why I idolised my mum; she was constant and loving. My father was erratic, moody and difficult to please. I remember that when he would come home from the pub, if the kitchen did not have the one specific item he wanted to eat in it, he would destroy all the food, throwing it onto the floor in a rage before heading off to bed and leaving my mother to clean it up and work out how she was going to feed her children the following day. At this point I have to say that we never went without food; I know mum went without to make sure we had what we needed. I am told that if dad was needed because there was a crisis at home someone was sent to the pub to retrieve him. I can also remember on many occasions I would climb under the table in the sitting room and pull the chairs in around me…my fortress…my safe haven when dad was ranting and raving, breaking things, arguing. I also hid in my fortress from the 'rag and bone' man. We don't seem to have 'rag and bone' men nowadays. They used to come around the streets ringing a bell and shouting 'rag and bone'…they were wanting to collect scrap metal and other objects they could make some money from. I can't remember who used to tell me but I believed the 'rag and bone' man could take me away. So that dining table was a little girl's solace on numerous occasions. My parents argued quite a lot in my early years; I remember one argument very clearly. It ended with my mother throwing the rent book at my father and telling him he could have it all and do it all…that she was going. I remember she got her shoes on and picked up her handbag and she left; to my great relief she only went to the local shop for cigarettes and therefore returned soon after. I dreaded my mother actually carrying out her threat to leave; I sure didn't want to be left behind. In my childlike understanding my mother wanted me and my father did not. It never ceases to amaze me how clever children can be as I quickly developed a plan to keep my mum from leaving when I felt she was about to. I would run and fetch the hairbrush and ask her to brush my hair for me; in my childlike thinking I had worked out that if mum was brushing my hair she couldn't physically leave and often as she brushed she would calm down.

Checking

Mamma, please don't leave me here on my own.
Please, I am willing and wishing and hoping you'll come home.
Please don't leave me here with him.
In his presence I am a nothing.
Do you know I sit on the stairs in the dark
& I watch the street all silent and stark,
& I wait and I watch for you to come?
Please don't leave this little girl, mum.
I think that you will be coming back;
I've done my check, you see.
All your clothes are in the wardrobe still
So I think you will be coming home to me.
Please don't leave me, mamma; I need you to come home.
Please don't leave me, mamma; I feel so very alone.

I don't think my parents had any idea about the damage these arguments and tension had on us children. They certainly never tried to keep it away from us and out of earshot; we always seemed to be in the middle of it somehow, which is why I liked hiding under the table. Although, I am told that mum on occasions did gather us children up and take us out for hours on end, bringing us home when she thought dad would be sleeping off the alcohol. Research by the charity Women's Aid states that children who live in domestic violence are at increased risk from emotional trauma, behavioural problems and mental health difficulties in later life. I always knew that it had affected me on some levels growing up, but even I was surprised when I found myself painting the following picture in an art therapy session over 20 years later...

Kate Swift

'My Fortress'
Painted in Art Therapy

From under the table I would hear you shout,
Too young to know what you are shouting about.
I pull the chairs in around me.
Under the table is my safety.
Sheltered from the battle zone,
Screaming adults banging and crashing in my
home.
Under the safety of my table I am okay,
Waiting for silence, waiting to come out and play.

Come save me from this life I know,
Where mamma shouts that she will go
& dad makes me feel like I'm not wanted at all.
Come save me from this crushing fall.

Come save me from this life I'm living here,
Where dad rants and raves and makes me fear.
The arguing and the stress: 'You have the kids; you
have it all.

Nobody's Rag Doll

I'm going', mamma declares, and I fall.

Come save me from this life my little girl is in.
Used and abused, drowning in other people's sin.
Punched and smacked, lost and alone
In a battlefield others call home.

Come save me from this life I was born into.
Where dad declared 'I'll bloody kill you".
No daddy here, just an angry man who shouts,
& a little girl who screams inside…
WILL SOMEONE LET ME OUT?

I cannot recall a single cuddle from my dad, but in his good moods he could be very funny. Dad does have a brilliant sense of humour which when it shines through always makes you laugh. My fondest childhood memory of my dad is that of standing on his feet, dad holding onto my hands, and he would walk me around the house. I was taking giant steps and it was such fun; I loved it. Another time he arrived home with a giant tube…he told me it was a giant tube of Smarties. It was in fact a paddling pool, light blue in colour with seats at the corners. We had a lot of fun in the paddling pool, us kids. As a child I always had long hair and my mum often put it into pig tails for me; dad used to hold my pig tails and call them handle bars for a bike. In these last few sentences are the sum total of my positive memories of having a father in my life. I still don't feel like I ever had a daddy…to me a daddy plays with you, spends time with you, cuddles you, makes you feel safe and nurtured, cherished and wanted. Dad's moods made life quite difficult in the house. If for instance he wanted peace and quiet because he had a headache, he would sometimes turn the electric off at the mains. My mother would be out and we just had to either go to bed or wait until someone turned it back on. I used to sit outside on the doorstep because I was really afraid of the dark. The street light made it brighter outside than inside the house. I was afraid of dad when he was in a mood, although he didn't hit the girls; he used to hit the boys sometimes but not the girls. I do recall one occasion when he dragged me down the stairs by my hair, but other than this one incident dad ruled with his moods and his voice. The only time we ever sat and ate together as a whole family was on two days in a year...Christmas day and Boxing Day. I think it is lovely to sit around the table and share a meal together. Even now when I go to dinner with my friend, her husband and son I really enjoy that time around the table together. I don't know what it is about it; I guess a feeling of belonging and unity. Although, in our house, it is probably just as well we didn't do that as it would have been anything but peaceful and united!

When I was approximately four to five years old I was playing in the garden on my own, on my little plastic horse. We had a large family dog that came bounding past me and knocked me clean into the pond. I would not be here today had our next door neighbour not heard the splash, scrambled over the fence and got me out. My parents were unaware of the drama in the garden. I do remember I got a bath and a nice cup of warm sugar milk...mmmhhh sugar milk! Hot milk with sugar to sweeten it; I loved it when I was a small child. The other thing I was crazy about as a child were soft toys! I had so many soft toys there wasn't room for me in the bed. My sister to this day still tells me I always picked – THE – ugliest soft toy out of the bunch. I always loved the ones with a fault even more than the rest. I would spend hours in my bedroom playing schools. All the soft toys would become the children in my class. Right from being a young child I wanted to work with children in a school when I was older. Looking back now I think it was because school was very happy and safe for me. I also loved playing with my doll and making mud pies in the garden! I still have some of my soft toys, dolls and my recorder from when I was small. I loved playing my recorder…the rest of the house didn't share my passion for it, however, and I was often sent to the bottom of the back garden to play it. Or a piece of it would vanish for months at a time; my sister would hide it to keep me quiet. I guess none of them heard what I thought I did. Just a few houses along from ours lived a young family and we used to play together. Looking back as an adult I'm sure those children were left home alone sometimes. The little boy always came to our house and said 'I'm hungry', and my dad nicknamed him 'hungry'; to this day I can't recall his proper name. My dad used to feed him on biscuits. There are several things I wish I still had now from my early years, like my dolls pram and my big yellow teapot. I would love to have these reminders of the more happy times of my early years. When I ask my mother what happened to all our things she just tells me she doesn't know. I think they got thrown away as we outgrew them. I feel sad that nobody thought to keep anything; I think it's lovely to have a few things from your childhood. I do have a tee-shirt that was mine and occasionally I get it out and unfold it, and then I think...'yes, I really was that little girl'.

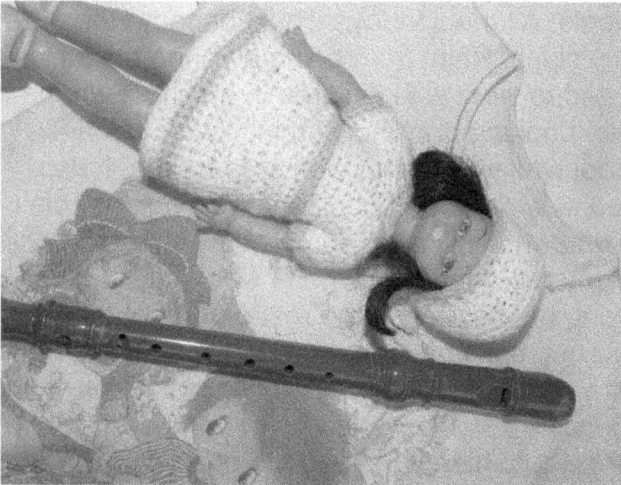

When I was five years old my dad had a very serious illness which almost cost him his life. He was in hospital for a long time and my mother visited him every single day as well as juggling caring for us kids. We were usually collected from school by family friends and my mum would collect us from there later in the evening. In that respect I don't know how my mum managed it...she kept us going and she nursed my dad back to as full a health as was now possible. His illness stopped the business and the drinking but it didn't stop the moody man who wanted us most of the time to be quiet. Looking back I wonder why my parents had such a large family; my dad was not what you could call a typical family man. However, they remained together and my mum juggled caring for all of us as best she could. It sounds like an awful thing to say now but I actually used to hope my dad was someone else! I always thought I'd be quite happy to belong to someone else because I always from very young felt that my own dad didn't want me and didn't love me. However, I am in no doubt of my parentage. I look at the photographs I do have of me and my siblings when we were little and I see innocent children. I look at the photographs of myself and I can see a sweet little girl who was almost destroyed. My mother has told me before that she was planning to leave my dad and then he got extremely sick and everyone around her told her she couldn't possibly leave him then…but how would life have been if she had? Maybe it would have been so much the better, and maybe it could have been somehow worse…I'll never know.

Now I am older I can see that this setting was a very opportunistic one for a man who wanted to befriend a family. A man disguised as a kind, gentle, caring person; very patient, good with the children, helpful around the house…and someone who read and quoted the word of God daily. I would have been around six years old when Mr X was introduced to the family via our neighbours. My mum was obviously flattered by the attention and glad of some help with the chores and the children. I remember Mr X spent a lot of time at our house, in between periods back in Northern Ireland where he was originally from. He would take us children on outings; I remember we went to see 'The Never Ending Story' at the cinema. All these years later it seems such a cruel irony that the film is about a book which speaks of a force called 'The Nothing'. It was like a darkness that ate up everything around it. There we were four children (My two oldest siblings had left home.), sitting watching that film with a man who was waiting to be a dark force in the lives of my brothers. As innocent children we had no idea what was sweeping into our young lives. As a young girl, I remember, I liked Mr X very much, whilst I did not view him as my dad; I already had one of those. He did some of the things my dad had never done, spent time with us, and made us feel important and special. At the time it was never apparent to me that he liked the boys more than us girls. I just thought I wasn't allowed to join in certain activities because I was too young. I can recall very clearly the night Mr X and my brothers camped out in the back garden in a tent. I can remember I desperately wanted to be able to stay in the tent – it seemed like such a fun thing to do when I was seven – it seemed like I was missing out on some of the fun. I remember I stayed up as late as possible hoping I would be allowed to go 'camping' too but I wasn't. Years later as a grown woman I now know what happened during that 'camping' trip and subsequent others. In our teens it was disclosed that Mr X had in fact sexually abused both of the two youngest boys. Looking back now I can see how he did prefer the boys, and how he only wanted them to be with him in the tent at night. He also took them away on a 'holiday', and I don't even want to imagine what happened during that time. But the facts in the cold, hard light of day all these years on is that Mr X had already served time for abusing his own children back in Northern Ireland and he went on to work his way into our family and abuse both of my brothers. And although he never abused me, I now feel like he did in a way, because he robbed us of our normality…and he set down the foundations of further abuse in the future. I also have to deal with the memories of our time with him as children, knowing what I now know about this man. I have photographs with a doll and teddies in them that were brought by him or sent to me from his mother back in Northern Ireland. I can also recall he took me and my other brother Charlie away – I think it was for a weekend – I can't imagine me going for any longer. I hated being separated from my mum when I was a child; I was such a mummy's girl, and she was my world. I don't remember where we went but we stayed in a caravan with a lady called Margaret. I think I slept in a room with Margaret and my brother Charlie was in a room with Mr X. They took me out and bought me a pretty dress to go out to dinner in the evening; again, I have a photograph of me wearing that dress. I remember Charlie arguing with Mr X and walking off; he was gone quite some time – or it seemed to be. On the drive back to London they stopped and bought me a big, cuddly toy. It is strange I don't know what happened as to why Mr X was not visiting us anymore. However, I can remember my mother sitting us all on the sofa, and we had to listen whilst she read letters out from him. He would write individual messages for us and quote the Bible. They were really beautiful looking letters; he could write in calligraphy, although these were in his own handwriting, and his drawings were very pretty too…but I now know these letters were from a man who was serving time in prison for crimes against his children. Many people in society think that they would know a 'bad' man or woman, but people who set out to abuse children are usually the kindest, nicest, most helpful people you can meet. If they were the kind of person you would not like or want to spend any time around this would not in most instances gain them access to children. I never did know what happened to Mr X, although he appeared on the scene a few more times as I was growing up; Charlie would take me to where he was living to visit, not many times, though. It is difficult now to see the photographs and to remember those times when Mr X was in our young lives, with the knowledge I now have as a grown woman. As I mentioned at the start of this chapter, I can now see that our family was the 'perfect' family for an abuser to gain access to. There were emotional and practical needs not being met, a role he could slot into and most of all, there were fairly vulnerable children that he would have seen as his prize. Children that were in need of attention and in the main, only getting what could be spared by their mother. Children who would have soaked up Mr X's attention, therefore, like little sponges in need of nurturing, because all children need to be nurtured, loved and cherished.

I believe that Charlie has paid very dearly for the abuse he suffered at the hands of Mr X and we, as his family, have paid with him. Charlie went down the route of finding ways to self-destruct and to self-medicate to escape the inner pain. Charlie was very disruptive at primary school and the local authority decided to send him to a boarding school for boys. I can still feel the sadness I felt the day I knew my brother had to go away. Charlie is a favourite brother of mine! I remember sitting on the stairs and feeling so very sad. As a young lad, on returning from boarding school he began glue sniffing, moved on to sniffing petrol and then from softer drugs to Heroin. I do not for one moment condone his drug taking or his behaviour because of it; I am very anti-drugs because of what I have seen. I spent my 16th birthday visiting Charlie in a young offenders institute. In fact I have been to several prisons and I never want to go to another one. Prison visiting is horrible in my opinion; the high fences/walls feel oppressive, and the personal searches you have to go through just to visit feel invasive. Although, I totally understand why these searches are necessary within our prisons. In some way you end up feeling like you have done something wrong yourself. Then at the end of the visit you have to walk away and leave someone you love behind. I couldn't comprehend why Charlie did not seem to want more from his life. Seeing children visiting their parent was particularly moving. I really felt for those children; prison is no place for little ones. I found it all very difficult and I reached a point where I just could not face it any longer. I went to visit Charlie one particular day; we had travelled for around three hours to see him. I got out of the car and I began to cry; I found it very hard to stop and from that day onwards I vowed I would never step inside another prison visiting hall. I told Charlie if he wanted to see me he would have to stay out of trouble because if he went to prison he would not be seeing me for the duration of his sentence…although I always sent letters and cards. Did it hurt that I felt he didn't love me enough to stay out of prison…? Yes, it did. But the grip of addiction is all-consuming. Thankfully these days I don't have to lose my brother to prison. Charlie has walked a very difficult path and one not entirely of his own making. Which means as his sister I have been exposed to much of that journey with him. I have an old Christmas photograph of myself playing my new music keyboard…I didn't have it for very long, as one of Charlie's friends took it to sell for money to buy a fix. In fact many things 'vanished' in our house over the years. I remember one time my mother came home having seen some of her ornaments in a local shop window for sale…yes, Charlie had taken them and sold them to the shop for money. I am pleased to say with baited breath that Charlie has in the last few years begun to turn his life around. What I would like to see, but I doubt very much if I ever will, is Mr X paying for what he did to both Charlie and Joe. I don't even know if he is still alive or where he is but I cannot allow that to drain my energy; the most important thing to me is that Charlie is okay; I love him very much. Some would say that Joe has paid a high price too, but I don't believe what he did, following on from his own abuse at the hands of Mr X, can ever be excused. Charlie's life of addiction is something which I have never felt comfortable talking about. Some people, understandably, have very strong views on illegal drugs, as do I myself. I had always felt it was partly my shame to carry but now I know that it is not. Indeed, reading this chapter will be news to some of my closest friends and I do feel a slight twinge of concern as to how people will respond and feel about it. However, in this book I am dealing in truths. Living and growing up with Charlie's addiction has been very painful at times. Watching it unfold and often descend into chaos was another very strong message to me as a child that the world could be a very scary place that I had no control over. It was not unusual for the police to be calling round to our house when Charlie was younger…lots of petty crime to feed that ravenous drug habit. I have to say I saw no benefit in locking Charlie away other than obviously he couldn't commit further crime, which of course matters…but there was no rehabilitation. Drugs are in our prisons and at times almost as readily available as on the outside. The Christmas day phone call from prison was always so hard. One of the most painful things he ever admitted to me was that he would sell the shoes off his feet for a fix. Many times I feared that Charlie would be found dead somewhere, particularly as some of his acquaintances have died through heroin overdoses and drug-related violence. I would have a fairly regular bad dream in which Charlie would be doing the one thing I didn't want him to do because it was the one thing which seemed unsafe. One time Charlie was missing for three days and eventually my mother and I found him on a concrete stairwell fast asleep. His body was kind of twisted and his face was tinged a blue colour. If it hadn't been for his slight snoring we would have thought he was dead. Then there were other times when you could not help but be amused, even though it was just sad, because otherwise you would just forever be crying. I remember one morning at about 3 am when I went downstairs to get some water. Charlie was in the kitchen as high as a kite, wearing yellow washing up gloves, hand washing his jeans in the sink, cooking beans on toast at the same time, and totally oblivious to the time. Around 5 am I came back downstairs and Charlie had gone off out leaving the front door wide open; how long it had been left open I don't know.

The fifteen plus year cycle of going in and out of prisons was finally broken when Charlie was diagnosed and properly treated for Bipolar Disorder. It was another mighty battle to get Charlie the help he needed from the mental health services. Some of the staff on the wards brushed him aside because he was a 'drug addict'; one even told me as much...'nothing you can do with a drug addict here'. But my mother and I knew this time his behaviour was very different; it was like nothing we had ever seen in him before. Charlie would be insisting someone had telephoned him to go meet him at 3am...he would try to get out of the car whilst it was driving down a busy road...he would arrive at my flat at 2 – 3 – 4 am and act like it was the middle of the day. On one occasion he telephoned the police and told them he heard a gunshot; they even asked him if he was absolutely certain and, of course, he said he was. The next thing I knew was that I had armed police at my front door and I had to take them to one side and explain how ill he was. Thankfully they were very understanding; in fact the police were excellent during that time. Often the police are left to care for people who should be in the care of our mental health sector. Charlie finally got the right help and a proper diagnosis when I had insisted on a meeting at the hospital with the top consultant. I told her that which was my firm belief at that time…that if they did not do something to help Charlie and to keep him safe he would end up dead somewhere. I firmly believed that; I had been living with his totally erratic behaviour for weeks. The consultant looked quite shocked by my statement and then she asked me what I wanted to happen. I told her that I wanted him to be sectioned for his own safety and I also told her I wanted him to go to a different hospital! The following morning, Charlie met the consultant and was sectioned. It was very upsetting to see him sectioned, even though I was the person who had insisted on it. For years my brother had been taken away from me…boarding school, prison, and there was nothing I could do about it. Now here I was being the one sending him away, getting him locked away…but as hard as I cried I knew it was the best thing for him. As much as it hurts me I would do it again if it meant keeping him safe. Charlie was in a drug-induced psychosis and we had been left to try to manage it ourselves for too many weeks. I had always assumed that when someone was that unwell the help would be readily available, but in this instance I assumed wrong. We had to fight to get people to see past the addiction and to see that this man was very sick. Why do we have to fight the system for help when we need it the most?! I have never given up on Charlie and I never will. I have been furious with him and cried many tears over his behaviour but I won't give up on the damaged child inside the man. It is my firm belief that Mr X has left his mark on Charlie in a most destructive way. Yet still there is something endearing about Charlie, and a lot of the now elderly residents where I grew up are still very fond of him, even though he has been mischief with a capital 'M'. Charlie without drugs is very loving. I take heart in a guy who is now prison-free and living at least in physical freedom. It is my deepest desire, one day, to see him free internally too. But it is a personal choice and a commitment to making the changes you need to make. It has been a very difficult road to walk but thankfully we are seeing some light. Many survivors can fall into the trap of self-medicating, taking something to forget, taking something to make them happy, taking something to just make it through the day. Whilst I myself have never touched a single drug, I have at times been able to understand that desire to take something or drink something to make it all go away. I have always known that this is not the answer; it is a quick fix which inevitably causes more problems than it could ever mend.

Nobody's Rag Doll

I hope for every time he puts a needle in his
arm…you feel a stab of pain.
I hope for every time he injects to forget what you
did…you remember it with shame.
I hope for every time he manages to escape
you…you are imprisoned in your mind.
I hope for every time he finds some peace…you
are faced with everything unkind.
When you abused that little boy…you may as well
have placed a needle in his hand.
When you abused that little boy…you took him to a
world man does not understand.
When you abused that little boy…you played a
game with his head.
When you abused that little boy…you left his
prospects dying fast and dead.
I hope for every time he denies the needle…he will
grow stronger.
I hope for every time he forgets with heroin…he
forgets what you did for longer.
I hope for every time he finds joy without a needled
high…you suffer in some way.
I hope for every time he resists his 'demons'…they
take you to hell to pay.

~

I will follow you…
I will follow you down this pathway to who knows
where.
I will follow you over broken glass.
I will follow you over broken dreams.
I will follow you over broken years.

Kate Swift

I will follow you down this pathway to who knows
where.
I will follow you until one day you turn back and
take my hand.

~

There is no funeral.
He is not physically dead.
But he lies screaming.
Dying inside my head.
On a grave I picture his name.
Lost in some cemetery.
Does that sound so insane?

~

Day after day you drown before my eyes.
I watch the tragedy on repeat whilst my heart
silently cries.
Day after day you spend time in crisis.
I watch and I wonder why your life is this.
Day after day I seek you in the desert of your
disease.
& I call for you to come on home...for we are both
so alone.

~

All you want.
All you think of.
All you crave.
All you ache for.
All you desire.

All you need.
A little white bag of powder.

~

Faded Hope

I don't want to bury you, don't want to lay you in the ground.
I don't want to kiss your life goodbye before real life you've found.
I don't want to get a phone call one day.
I don't want to be told that drugs have stolen you away.
I don't want to identify you in some cold mortuary.
I don't want to be living with this possibility.

I love you, brother of mine.
I think drug-free you are a person mighty fine.
I miss you when you are locked up inside.
How I've missed you and how I've cried.
I don't want to identify you in some cold mortuary.
I want my brother beside me.

~

The dregs of your society.
A drain on the system, a drain on money.
The nightmare of your job.
To you it's another no-good junkie on the rob.
'Lock them up'; that is what you cry.
Leave them in the gutter to shoot up and die.

Dreg of society…NO…brother of mine.

Kate Swift

Breaking my heart with your relentless life of crime.
Pushing the boundaries so far and wide.
Tearing me apart inside.
Can anyone, anything rescue you?
Dreg of society…NO…brother of mine: see what
you do?

~

Hope in Hell

You must want more from your life than this.
You must have dreamt of something: ever made a
wish?
This cannot be enough for you.
Living to get high every day.
Is that really all you want to do?
What goes through your mind in a prison cell at
night?
Do you want to make things right?
You must want more from your life than this.
For you I am dreaming a dream.
For you I'm holding out for miracles.
For you I'm making my wish.

~

So now let me take you back to that perfect summer's day, to eight-year-old me, curled up on the sofa watching cartoons on the television. I was aware of the milkman outside, the familiar humming of the milk float and clinking of the bottles. The washing machine was whirring in the kitchen and mum was back and forth pegging out the washing. My older brother Joe was lying on the floor in front of the television; this was his favourite spot. Until he stood up and walked over to where I was on the sofa: he told me to move over and he sat down on the edge of the sofa. Then he touched me in a place and in a way that I had never been touched before. I remember it so clearly, more clearly than I would like to remember it, if I am honest. I cannot recall what either he or I did directly afterwards. I knew I had to be 'normal', and I somehow knew it was not something to be spoken about. Other than telling me to move over it was done without words. This was where my life as I had known it to this point would change forever, with something that lasted just a few minutes that first time. Here began the sexual abuse which was to scar my life for many years to come.

Life was 'normal' outside of the abusive episodes. I was enjoying school; my make-believe games with my dolls and stuffed toys kept me entertained for hours. I loved drawing and colouring. I loved spending time with my mum but she was often busy or stressed out with something or another. My favourite spot was sitting as close to my mum as possible. I would sit down on the carpet by her legs and sometimes she would play with my hair, which

I loved. Sometimes I played hopscotch in the garden with my sister, but mostly we fought like cat and dog. We shared a bedroom, she and I; it was that girly shade of pink and not very big, enough room for two single beds, furniture, and then not much space in the middle. The curtains were white with pink daisy style flowers on. One time I remember we fell out and divided up the bedroom; my sister declared her half of the room and told me proudly that I wouldn't be able to enter or exit as the door was on her half! We even went as far as to put tape down the middle! It was very much a love/hate relationship, but as I said she was very much a daddy's girl and I was always a mummy's girl. She would defend dad and I would always defend mum, in everything. As we have grown into adults our relationship hasn't improved that much. I have gone for more than a year choosing not to see her because she has at times been extremely spiteful. We just seem to always have a very short fuse between us.

My best friend Sophie was always a solid, warm and loving friend. We met at primary school and we remain close friends. Sophie spent a lot of time at my house and she quickly became part of the family. In fact we both have great affection for each other's families. Sophie's grandparents always referred to me as 'Sophie's little friend round the corner' because we did live that close. I refer to her grandparents as 'Nan' and 'Granddad'; they are 'salt of the earth' types of people. Sophie is such a gift to me; she understands each individual person in my family like no one else I know. Some of my happiest memories, in fact many of my happiest memories, are times Sophie and I spent together. One of our favourite pursuits in the summer was to build a camp in the garden and spend the night outside…although often we would give in at some unearthly hour and creep back into the house! We were never ones to be beaten, though: we would be back out making a fire to cook breakfast. Actually, come to think of it, I wonder if that's part of the reason why Sophie is now vegetarian! The hours we spent trying to cook our breakfast…and even scarier is the fact that we consumed it too! One of our other favourite pastimes was cooking up a storm (quite literally in some cases) in the kitchen. I will never forget, in our teens after one of our cook ups, being in the home economics lesson the following morning and the teacher announcing the Salmonella Crisis with the eggs…I and Sophie were mortified remembering the scrambled egg we had consumed the night before, and both decided there and then we may be coming to a sticky end! We would come home from school and then spend an hour or longer on the phone chatting to each other. Much to the bewilderment of Sophie's dad, who couldn't begin to imagine what we could possibly find to say to each other after a day at school together! But following a day at school…a long chat on the phone…Sophie would often come to my house for a few hours in the evening. Sophie was and is a big part of my life. Through my childhood and teens she was the solid friend I needed. I never told her about the abuse; we just had fun together, normal children doing normal things, and I'm so glad for that. Today there are lots

of things I cannot recall from those years and
Sophie is like a memory bank; she reminds me of
happy times or funny moments I have long
forgotten. I think memories got lost as I tried to
blank out the horrible parts of my life.

~

Sarah

I found your doll, Sarah with blue eyes and blonde
hair.
I remember you with her in the garden; you were
happy there.
Playing 'house' in the sunshine as contented as
can be.
Do you remember?
Can you see?
The games you played for hours on end.
That doll was a dear friend.

When you played in the garden nothing bad
happened to you.
There was nothing out there he could do.
You see, Sarah – she belongs to an innocent child.
Pure and undefiled.
The arms that carried that doll did nothing wrong.
The arms that carried that doll were little and not
strong.

The child who owned that doll liked taking care of
her real good.
She liked to dress her, hug her, brush her hair and

do all the nice things she could.
Because the owner of the doll was loving and kind,
Her games of make believe were typical in a child's
mind.
Mother and baby in a happy, sunny world.
Child contented and lovingly held.

The owner of Sarah should have had and felt all
those loving things too, you know.
But unlike Sarah she lived in the real world and had
to grow.
& unlike Sarah she had to live with abuse.
She had real feelings and knew ill-use.
But the owner of Sarah was as innocent as can be.
Won't you look at Sarah, maybe hold her once
more.
Remember the little girl and then BELIEVE ME.

~

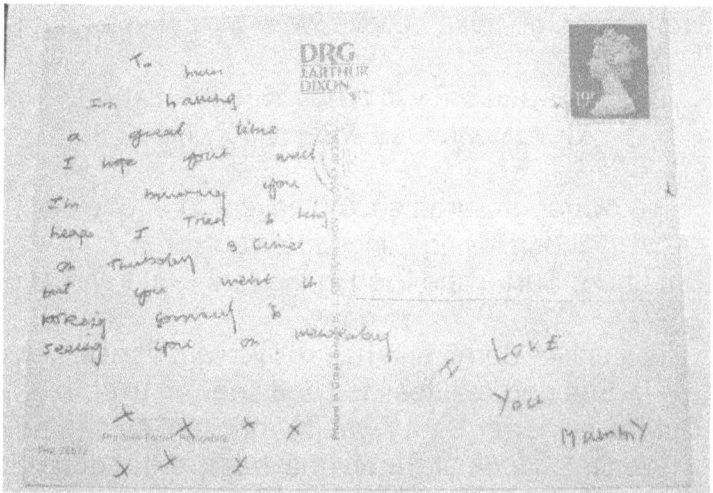

(A postcard I sent from Girl Guide Camp)
The postcard reads...'To mum, I'm having a great
time. I hope your well. I'm missing you heaps. I
tried to ring on Thursday 8 times but you weren't in.
Looking forward to seeing you on Wednesday'

My Girl Guide Badges

The second time I was aware of being abused was in my bed. In those early months/years of the abuse I would be woken from my sleep by Joe trying to climb into my bed with me sometime during the night. Sometimes I would try to push him away and other times I was too tired, too sleepy, too startled, or conscious of not waking the house, to fight. He would take what he wanted from me, always saying very little or nothing. Always just standing up and walking away afterwards. I used to pull the quilt up around me tight, sometimes over my head, so I could cry myself back to sleep. I have always wondered if my sister knew and if she was also abused before me. I am not aware of her being abused but sometimes she reminds me of someone who has been abused.

The morning would bring daylight and a sense of relief. A new day could begin again and I knew I needed to just be myself. Even at the age of eight, I knew it was not something anyone must ever know. The way in which it was done, the timing and the silent threat, bought my silence for many years to come. Mostly in the early days the abuse consisted of touching and of being forced (my wrist gripped by his hand and placed on his genitals). Even now after all the therapy I have had, all the work I have done on healing and making peace, it makes me feel physically sick to describe the details. The abuse would happen sometimes night after night, but then it would stop for some weeks and I would dare to think it was over. Just as it stopped without rhyme or reason it would begin again.

'Where is my sun?' the little girl said.
All of the lights have gone out inside my head.
Where is the warmth; I'm feeling so bitterly cold.
Nobody to hug me and no hand to hold.
Where is my smile?
It faded away too soon.
I see only darkness now, no stars or a brilliant moon.
Where is the little girl I was yesterday?
Before he stole my sunshine away.

~

Looking back now I can see there were possible signs that someone may have been able to pick up on. If they could they never did for whatever reasons. I had terrible nighttime terrors and

nightmares. I would be lying in my bed and literally imagine all these images all around the walls. A re-occurring nightmare I had was about the windows in my bedroom: a man with large wings would be outside the window beating on them to get in. I hated night-times all round; I hated the dark, the abuse, and the nightmares. I would always avoid going to bed for as long as possible: most of us do, don't we?! We want to stay up and be where the action is or see something on television. For me, I just did not want to go up to bed. If I fell asleep in the sitting room and someone woke me I would jump and be very startled. I hated going up to bed on my own, so if there were no lights on upstairs I would make my dad go up first, and I had a routine he had to follow: he had to put the landing and bedroom light on, check the windows were shut tight, draw the curtains leaving not a single gap in them, and then before I went to bed I would check the wardrobe! When I think about that now I see a young girl who was trying to be safe, trying to shut out the dangers, but the predator was inside the house…the predator was her older brother and no amount of bedtime checks were going to cancel him out.

Kate Swift

The Bedtime Monsters

Time for the bedtime ritual before sleep.
Curtains had to be shut tight, no tiny gap to peep.
Check inside the wardrobe, nothing nasty hiding
under there.
Looking for signs of danger under the bed and
everywhere.
Is she safely tucked into bed now for the night?
All snug and safe, warm and protected inside.
We checked all the places where the monsters
could hide.
But we missed the monster disguised as 'family'.
We missed her greatest threat from which she is
not free.
As safe as houses, a child in her home, in her bed.
Listening for that creaking floorboard.
The figure in the doorway she had come to dread.
This will be an ordinary night for her once again.
& tomorrow…tomorrow she will smile.
& silently choke on the pain.

~

It is hard to explain, but sometimes when we were
all downstairs in the sitting room watching
television, he would look at me in a certain way and
in that look I knew what he wanted. As I got older I
had two tricks for trying to avoid the abuse. Our
bathroom and toilet were downstairs and I
sometimes would insist I needed the bathroom until
he let me go; then I would stay down stairs for as
long as possible. Sometimes it worked and
sometimes he would come back later on. The other

was I'd insist I needed a glass of water but that one didn't work so well, worth a try, though. To the outside world, to our family, we were just 'normal' children, brother and sister. But it was anything but normal in his twisted desires and visits to my bed. I remember at school he would get into fights sometimes; he was known as someone not to be messed with. Quite fierce tempers even then, I remember the day he punched his fist through the sitting room door and I remember his exact words to our mother. He said, 'It was her head or the door'. I can't remember what I had done.

In our house the males were top of the pecking order. My sister and I would usually be given our dinner to eat in the kitchen, whilst the boys ate at the table in the sitting room with dad. Joe always watched television lying on the carpet right in front of it and it did feel like he was quite dominant. Dad certainly always seemed to prefer any of my other siblings to me. He and Joe would often have a laugh at other people's expense; they wouldn't laugh with you but at you. To this day I have a thing about people laughing at you or with you. They are two very different things; one brings a shared joy and the other a sense of humiliation for the one being laughed at. I never really knew why my dad didn't like me, but I often felt that he didn't like me. My mother said he always resented the extra time and attention I needed as a sick baby going through the operation. I really don't know if it was that or something else. Sophie's dad seemed the total opposite to mine; I'm sure she won't mind me saying that she and her dad are very close.

Sophie's dad was interested, protective, involved. You could argue that my father was an unhealthy man, which is not untrue…but prior to the illness he was a drinker…so never a 'daddy'. I remember in senior school when the other girls used to complain about their dads not letting them do something, such as stay out late or go somewhere. I used to wish my dad was like that! For me it would have shown me that he cared enough to put the boundaries down and he wanted to be protective of his daughter. I guess our mother was the active parent and in many ways like a single parent, as she often cared for dad and us kids. We never had a family holiday. Days out were mostly trips to the parks with a picnic…countless sandwiches, a large bottle of Cherryade and lots of walking to tire us out! We used to love the boxes of broken biscuits you could buy; I don't know if you can still buy them now. We used to get the bottles of fizzy drinks from the milkman…and if you returned the empty bottle you got ten pence back again! On Sundays mum always cooked a roast dinner and everyone was expected to be there for dinner at 1pm. That was probably the closest we got to being a connected family. Sunday dinners stopped shortly after I turned twenty-one. That's when mum announced that she had done her job…raised the children, and now was going to do more what she wanted to do. On my 21st birthday she was out doing her own thing when I thought she was going to spend some time with me. At times it almost felt like mum wanted to be a single woman again with no ties, and although all her children were grown up at this point, I think your children are always your children.

Perhaps you are needed to a lesser degree...but as a parent you are still needed. I had always just loved time spent with my mum; I didn't mind where we were when I was with her. Sometimes we would go to the local cemetery together; seems a strange place to go but we would throw monkey nuts down for the squirrels. Then we would sit very still and watch them all come out to feed, which gave us both a lot of pleasure. Apparently as a small girl I called them 'Scribbles'!

I can't help but wonder now if we had been taught at school or by our parents about child sexual abuse…would we be in a very different place in our lives? At school we are taught about road safety and stranger danger. We learn about the dangers of fireworks and not to play with matches. Why, oh, why are our children not taught about 'safe' touch and 'bad' touch? Some people are alarmed when I say this but children don't have to be made frightened; there are ways of appropriately teaching our children that their body is special and if someone ever tries to touch it in certain places that is not allowed. We need to empower our children to know the threat of child abuse. Empower them with knowledge and make sure they know they can TELL if something did happen to them. We go to great lengths to protect our children from all sorts of dangers as they grow up: we teach them healthy eating, to take care of their teeth etc…and yet we don't talk about a threat that takes place for one in every four people…in fact that statistic is probably much higher in reality now.

Telling was not something I ever considered until later in my teens when circumstances left me feeling I had no other choice but to say something to somebody. You are locked in this secret void; the abuse is often in silence or with verbal threats issued. The abuser always picks their moment very carefully; you are aware that they would not want anyone else to know. Because you are made to be a very active part of what is happening, the shame binds you into silence. I know from an early age I thought I would be in so much trouble if my mother found out what had happened. I should have been able to tell her what was happening to me, but for the reasons I have explained above and all the complex thoughts and feelings that go with this type of abuse, I could not. I carried my secret like an invisible millstone around my neck. In the times when the abuse ceased happening I would feel such great relief and dare to allow hope to creep in that it had stopped. That was all I wanted…I wanted it to stop but it would always begin again. Sometimes when I was mischievous in the way that all children can be, my mother would tell me off and then she would send me away from her. I still can hear her saying what she always said to me: "You're a bad girl and I only like good girls". I remember finding that so very confusing and frustrating. I hated being told to go away from her, and also I remember I desperately wanted to be a 'good girl' and I just felt like I did not know how to be one. Now, with my adult head, I can see that I was a 'normal' child and the labels added to me of being a 'bad girl' were unjust. I now understand why I couldn't reach that unreachable goal of being my mother's good girl because in the main I already was. I felt very little warmth and approval from my dad so that made my mother's approval all the more important to me, and I sought it endlessly at times.

We were not smacked a lot as children by any means but I can remember just occasionally my mother would really lose her temper. This was never helped by my fit of the giggles I got when I was really nervous, and for her to think I was merely laughing at her angered her more. These occasions ended in me or my sister being hit again and again in the corner of the room; I don't suppose it lasted very long at all but in my memory it feels like a long time. Even now it is difficult to tell that to you. It is difficult to criticise the woman I always adored, and adore her I did. However, through therapy I have learnt that it is okay to speak the truth. I don't believe we can just excuse poor parenting but I do think we can look at possible reasons why things went the way they did. That is not to say I believe you can just blame your past and repeat mistakes for your own children. One of my favourite sayings is 'When people know better they can do better'. The frustrating thing with my mother is she never wants to look over her shoulder. She lives very much in the here and now and refuses on the whole to discuss the past. For me, I believe that sometimes you have to go backwards and look at your past in order for you to be able to right some of the wrongs, make some peace inside of yourself and therefore go forwards. I don't know a lot about my family history; on my father's side I don't know any relations at all. On my mother's side I knew my Nan for a time when I was growing up, but she was not a well lady. Nan had Bipolar Disorder at a time when it was not as understood and well treated as it is now. My mother has spoken on a few occasions about being taken to visit her mum in the 'mental' hospital when the patients were placed on chairs all down the corridor. It makes me feel sad to think of my mum, then a little girl having to go to what must have been quite a scary scenario for one so young. Also to have to see her own mother in that very unwell state. When we were growing up it was a curious thing that my mum always had her own knife and fork to eat with, always. I never understood why until she told me in recent years that as a little girl nobody had explained her mother's illness to her and she thought she could catch it by eating from the same cutlery. How sad that nobody ever realised and corrected that for her and she had spent so long fearing she would catch her mother's Bipolar Disorder. When I think about my Nan's ill-health, I have a lot of compassion for my mum; I can't imagine she had much mothering. The only other relatives I had outside of the immediate family were my aunt and uncle whom I loved very much. But we didn't see them often, a few times a year.

So my primary school years ticked by and the abuse continued in pretty much the same pattern as I described. I never got used to being woken in the middle of the night by him. Mostly in those early years of the abuse it was all touching and trying to force my hand to touch him where he desired. It makes you feel so tainted, even as a young girl. I used to go down to the bathroom and splash myself with water afterwards. As we moved on up to Senior school the abuse became more physical, being pinned down, being told what to do; it stopped happening during the night-time but would happen at other times of the day, mostly evenings. I used to listen out for the loose floor board on the landing; I would hear first his door handle turn and then the floorboard creak, and I knew he was just outside the door. He would enter the room, and if I had music on he would walk straight to the music and turn it down before proceeding to do what he wanted to do with me. Often I was sitting at my desk doing homework or drawing and so he would walk up behind me. Sometimes I felt frozen to the chair; other times I would drink in every detail of the wall paper or the curtains, anything to focus on.

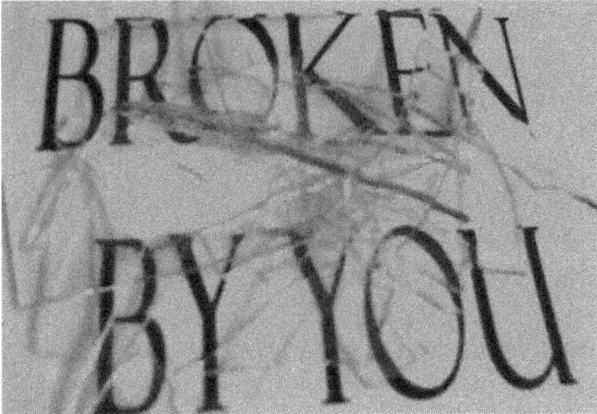

BROKEN BY YOU

The abuse wasn't kept to just the bedroom upstairs; sometimes if I was standing in the bathroom brushing my hair he would walk in and touch me, and the same in the kitchen. It was about opportunity; when he saw an opportunity he would mostly take it. He was always on guard during the whole episode, listening in case someone did suddenly walk up the stairs. Sometimes he would stop what he was doing for a moment and almost like freeze-frame it to listen if he thought he heard something. I can't explain how it felt to have his weight on top of me and his breath on my face…it felt suffocating. I hated having my clothes undone, and I hated even more having my hand physically forced against his body. By the time I was into my teens the abuse was everything from a grope to rape. Many times over I was pinned down, or trapped underneath him, and still sometimes now I have days where I have pain in my wrists. I don't think the pain is related to back then but it takes me right back to that time because the pain is the same. The ways in which he physically pinned me down and restricted me were nothing compared to how pinned down and restricted I felt internally. When he turned and silently walked away leaving me in a state of undress wherever it was he wanted me, it takes everything to pick yourself up and switch back to 'normal' mode…after all you might soon be being called for dinner or some other everyday thing. That is where I saw myself as a rag doll…his rag doll. I felt like an object to be picked up, used and left on the floor like discarded rubbish. I was a rag doll who always wanted to be the princess.

Drawing by Gemma Merrick
Created especially for 'Nobody's Rag Doll'

Many times I had 'why and what if' on the tip of my
tongue but I would open my mouth and not a sound
would come out. I wanted to ask him...why me?
And also...what if I get pregnant? But I never once
managed to ask either of those questions.
Sometimes I would push him away repeatedly but
other times I felt tired and defeated. Sometimes I
just wanted to get it over with because if he didn't
get what he wanted he would try again later that
evening. I still used my old tricks of insisting I
needed the bathroom or that I needed some water;
sometimes it brought me some freedom. I
remember that during therapy I questioned myself

for a time…why did I be where he could abuse me…but I was in my home doing what was 'normal'…doing my homework, playing music, sleeping in my bed. Always when he got up and walked away he went to his bedroom, shut the door and stayed there for a while. Just as in the early days, the abuse would stop for a few weeks, maybe even a little longer, and I would every time dare to believe it was over. It was never over, even after I told it still wasn't finally over for one last time. The abuse made me feel dirty, cheap and worthless. I was forever a rag doll used and left on the floor alone, often in physical discomfort. The thing I always feared happening, that one of my parents would find out, did actually happen on one occasion and also two near misses. Once my mother walked into my bedroom to find him in my bed; she was SO furious with both of us and just screamed to never let her catch us in bed together again. Did she never think to speak to us about it separately? Did she really just scream at us and then forget it? I can only guess that she did because she never mentioned it again. For me it only served to confirm my worst fears that if she ever knew the truth I would be in so much trouble. I sure didn't want to be in any trouble, and least of all with my mum who I still idolised. Wouldn't you think that being caught like that might have stopped him in his tracks…the abuse continued but then I guess in his mind he had got away with it all but for a few moments of embarrassment. In my teens the role between parent and child was somewhat reversed between my mother and I. I would be the one sitting waiting at the landing window for mum to come home late at night or early hours of the morning. I would be the one questioning her when she did come home! Indeed mum often commented on the role reversal. As a teenager I still needed my mother but it was like she had decided I didn't really need her to be there. That fear I had as a very small child of her leaving me stayed with me throughout my childhood. Sometimes when I came home from school and my mum wasn't home, I would go up to her bedroom and check that her clothes were still in the wardrobe. I did that many times growing up and I remember the relief when I saw all her things in their rightful place. Then I just had to wait for her to come home; I knew she would but I didn't know when. It never occurred to me that she could have left and just left everything behind! I thought if she left I would be left behind but her personal belongings would be gone.

One of my most uncomfortable experiences abuse-related was at school. We were in a fairly small classroom being shown a sex education video; I felt physically sick and I asked to leave the room to use the bathroom, and then I stayed there for as long as I possibly could. I never felt like I fitted in at senior school and I never liked it like I did primary. I went to an all girls school, and teenage girls on the whole are interested in boys, make up, fashion etc. At least a lot of the ones I went to school with were! None of those things were me; I sure wasn't interested in boys. The only boy crush I had in my teens was a character from an American television programme. I sure didn't want any boys near me and I wasn't terribly interested in my appearance; in fact I should have really taken more care of myself than I did. I was never with the 'in' crowd of girls at school, always on the edge of things, or so I felt. I didn't like having male teachers other than our form tutor who was lovely. I was well behaved in school and mostly enjoyed learning. Apart from maths, which I was worse than hopeless at…myself, Sophie and a few others would sit at the back of the classroom and try to do as little as possible. The maths teacher eventually realised our lack of productivity in his lessons and began marking how many sums we had completed in a one hour lesson. Usually you could count how many with one hand! I really didn't like languages, either; my head felt scrambled enough without trying to learn another language. The following is an extract from my final school report which was written by my form tutor…

Kate is a kind, hardworking and totally unselfish person who will always help others in need…I am sure that Kate will always use her special skills and abilities to help aid others.

When I was fifteen years old that storm cloud which arrived in my life at the age of eight broke, and life was never going to be the same again. A lack of something had me very worried, and as the months ticked by I was beside myself. Seven months in total had gone by with nothing and I was almost convinced therefore that I was pregnant by him. My head became totally consumed by it. It was the last thing on my mind at night and the first thing the next morning. It was hell on earth, the fear and dread of the situation. The knowledge that my secret could no longer be a secret. Who to tell…and what was I going to say? Finding the words…what words do you use…stringing the sentence together…I felt like I didn't even know where to begin. It sounds so simple to put the sentence together but it was anything but simple. I was a mess inside my mind and I was feeling so depressed. I even remember wanting to just make 'it' go away, and I would press my stomach hard against things. I looked up about abortion clinics and racked my brain trying to think if I could actually go through with such an act. All of these were my runaway thoughts and I reached a point where I felt like I could take it no longer and I just HAD to tell someone something. I had once before been to see a doctor because I was experiencing a lot of chest pains. The Doctor suggested something may be troubling me perhaps, and said I should come back to see him with my parents…but of course that was the last thing I was going to do. I had a lot of chest pain through anxiety.

I first broke my silence to another school friend and she encouraged me to tell a teacher. I could not even speak the words; it ended up being a very small scribbled note on a piece of paper. The note said 'I think I am pregnant by my brother'; understandably so the teacher looked shocked and very concerned. It was the end of the school day; all the chairs were up on the desks, and she told me to go home and that she needed to speak to the head of the school. The following morning I had absolutely no idea of the ticking time bomb that awaited me as I walked to school that day. I was told at morning registration that the head teacher wanted to see me in her office immediately. When I got to her office she was very nice and she spoke to me about the possibility of being pregnant and got me to confirm what I had written in the note the day before. I remember she asked me to stand up and she looked at my tummy and told me that I didn't look like I was seven months pregnant. Then she telephoned the local clinic and arranged for me to go and have a test that afternoon. I was allowed to take a friend with me, and we both arrived at the clinic to discover we were right in the middle of the routine baby clinic. There were lots of mums with their babies in the waiting room and I felt so ashamed sitting there in my school uniform. Maybe they didn't assume anything but I felt like I was being judged as a 'silly' girl, another teen pregnancy. It felt like forever waiting to be called in to see the nurse…when she told me I was NOT pregnant I was very shocked, having been so convinced, and of course was extremely relieved. The nurse then proceeded to ask me how I came to think I was and about safe sex. Her face was one of horror when I told her the circumstances of me being stood in front of her that day. Looking back, words fail me when I think about how this was managed at the time. Why did I have to attend the clinic during a mother and baby session? Why was the nurse not made aware of the situation before my arrival? Perhaps in the urgency of the situation these points were not considered, but I have considered them many times since. The sense of relief as I walked back to school was immense; I had no idea what awaited me back in the head teacher's office on my return from the clinic.

I had to report straight back to the office and I told the head teacher my good news and she was pleased. However, she then told me that some other people were waiting in the other office to talk to me, and I just remember her opening the door and a room full of faces greeting me…social workers…child protection police officers etc. It was very daunting to say the least; they introduced themselves to me and talked over what needed to happen. They told me two social workers were that very afternoon at my home telling my mother about the sexual abuse. My father, due to his medical condition, couldn't retain information and therefore was not told anything at all. That was the first time I heard the words 'sexual abuse'; before then I never had a label for it. I had no idea that it had a name and it happened to many other children. This was a Friday and I was told that on the Monday at school I would need to talk to the child protection officers in a lot more detail. It was arranged that I would go and stay with my school friend for the weekend. At the end of the school day the social worker, who was a nice lady, drove me home to collect some things for the weekend. As we pulled up near my house my mother was standing outside on the pavement and she looked so crushed. I got out of the car and walked over to where she was standing. I had no idea what she was going to say to me. It is still a painful memory, seeing her for that first time after she knew. She looked at me, and all she kept saying to me was 'Tell me you're not pregnant', and I replied, 'I'm not', before scurrying inside to collect some things. My oldest brother was doing some DIY inside and he was angry and wanted to know why some social workers had come to the house. I knew it was not going to happen but I wanted my mum to be angry with Joe; I wanted her to rescue me; I wanted her to tell me that she still loved me. My friend's parents were kind, loving people and they had agreed to look after me for the weekend, and that is what they did. All weekend I was ever conscious that on Monday morning I had to speak about the sexual abuse in detail, and I was trying to prepare myself to be able to do just that. By the time Monday arrived I was feeling able to talk to the female child protection worker I had met on the Friday. However, when I got to the office the people were new ones apart from the social worker, and that was difficult. I gave my police statement with my dear English teacher holding my hand throughout; it took me over three hours to complete it. It was then decided that Joe and I could not live in the same house. My mother was given the decision by social services to decide which one of us would leave. I will always remember it; I can still see myself standing in the hallway just by the stairs. My mother looked at me and she said that I was stronger than Joe, that he needed her, and that I had more friends and would cope better. The rejection cut through my soul like an axe: that may sound over the top, but this was the woman I had adored right from my earliest memories. I never wanted to be with anyone else and in that moment I felt like Joe had somehow won, that he had got the one thing that meant everything to me. My life felt like it was splintered into a million little pieces: it was really devastating. My mother was always there for Charlie with his addiction and now she was there for Joe too. It felt like if you did something bad she loved you more. My mother felt rejected by me because I wouldn't discuss things with her, but is that any wonder given the responses and reactions I had got? She couldn't understand why I didn't just tell her... if only it was that simple. If children felt they could tell and that they would be believed and not blamed there would be less damage done. Where was my validation? Furthermore, she was furious with me that outside agencies were involved and she couldn't just sweep this under the carpet.

TOLD...
HORRIFIC,
SCARY,
SAD,
DIFFICULT.
TORMENT.
PANIC.

JUST...
A LOOK,
WORDS,
COMFORT,
KINDNESS,
VALIDATION,
HUGS.

BUT...

NOTHING.
SILENCE,
HURT,
BITTER
REJECTION,
ANGER.

~

At the point of needing to be fostered or placed into care I was very fortunate in that my friend's parents agreed I could stay with them and they would take care of me. I will be ever thankful for the kindness they showed me and the fact that they kept me from having to go into a totally strange new home. Also, I had my school friend there with me. Their house was only a short walk from my family home and I went home often; that was the only place I wanted to be because I wanted my family. My mother was extremely angry with me for a long time after the abuse disclosure. We had many heated words when I did go home. She was furious with me for bringing social workers into her life and more so that I did not tell her about the abuse. On one occasion she did actually ask me did I lie back and just think of England. That has to be the cruellest use of that phrase ever spoken and one again that I don't think I will ever forget. It is strange that although home was really hostile I still wanted to be there: I guess I wanted the familiarity when everything else felt shattered. I began skipping school so I could go and spend time at home when Joe would not be there. I remember one day when I was walking back up to my foster home: there was quite a busy road to cross, and I remember for a few minutes standing at the edge of the kerb willing myself to just walk out into the oncoming traffic. My foster family were lovely, kind people and it was no reflection on them the way I felt. I just wanted my family and I felt like it had been torn away from me, and I didn't know at that point if I would ever be returning home. I can remember feeling like a bag lady for some of the time; I was forever going back and forth with carrier bags of my belongings. Whilst fostered I had to go and stay somewhere else for a week whilst my foster family were away on holiday. (They had tried to change the booking to include me but were not able to.) My mother arranged for me to go and stay with a lady from the church for a few days and then another few days with another lady. However, the reasons she gave for me needing to stay were that I was arguing terribly with my sister and she needed to separate us. My sister was heavily pregnant with her first child at the time. Whilst I was staying with the second lady my sister had her son by emergency delivery. My new nephew was a very sick little boy and spent the first few weeks of his life in the baby intensive care unit. This resulted in me being given a talking to about saying sorry to my sister and being nicer when I returned home! Little did they know I was returning to my foster family and only staying with them because I was on the child protection register and not allowed to live at home! When my sister brought her baby home from the hospital he was also the subject of a case conference to determine if he was at any risk from Joe. I remember feeling really guilty that my sister had to go through that stress with her little baby. In hindsight of course it wasn't my fault but at the time I felt responsible because I had spoken out initially. I felt really sad not being able to be at home with my new baby nephew but I was in foster care for a further three months.

My mother would have said practically anything, I think, to maintain the charade to the outside world. I often got a sense that she was just desperate to have me home so that nothing was unusual to the outside world. One thing nobody ever knew was that I had sneaked one of my mother's jumpers to my foster home with me and often at night I would cuddle it close. I spent a lot of time feeling extremely angry with my mum but I never once stopped loving her.

When I was in school my mind was everywhere but where it should have been at the time. I was forever being called over to the head teacher's office and I quickly got labelled as head teacher's favourite, which opened me up to some bullying for that. How could I tell my fellow pupils the real reason I was always getting called away? I used to think 'If only they knew what it was really for'. One time it was to be taken to the local rape suite at the police station for a medical examination, but I just could not bring myself to do it. I had two female social workers, both of whom were nice people. Joe, when questioned by the police, admitted abusing me but also then disclosed the abuse he had suffered at the hands of Mr X all those years before, and that was the first I knew of it. I can't help but wonder if that is why my mother's reaction was about supporting him. Joe was bailed to return to the police station at a later date, where he was then given a caution. A caution for taking away my childhood…just a caution. I wish now in some ways that I was going through the police process as an adult in the place I am now in my mind. When those decisions were made I was a very traumatised teenager who wasn't able to be assertive and proactive about my case. I want to go back and ask why just a caution; I want someone to try to explain that to me…I don't think it can be justified. Joe was also required to complete some therapy sessions which he did in due course; I believe a total of just twelve sessions. Is that really adequate rehabilitation/punishment for someone who had abused for that many years? For someone who showed their victim no remorse. Is that really enough to ensure that this person is going to be safe around children in the future? When my first book was published earlier this year I finally felt heard and validated but it was not from the source it should have come from.

I was taken to a 'child guidance' clinic for some counselling but I did not want to go there and talk to yet another stranger. I was a very hurt and angry teenager who was tired of feeling like she had to do all these things. I didn't understand why I was there; I didn't understand at the time that it was to benefit me, and we had several standoffs in the waiting room as I refused to go into my session! Eventually I settled with one person there and I began some counselling. I was on the child protection register and regular case conferences were held. The first few I attended, I just remember a big, long wooden table and all these faces around it. Some of the faces I knew and some I did not. I remember the very first meeting because I tripped on the stairs. These were always so difficult and to me it felt like a room full of people making decisions for me. My mother was always either very angry or very tearful at these meetings. All my mother wanted was for things to return to 'normal'. Once before one of these case conferences I remember she turned to me and said 'Have you not got anything to say to save this family?' I was acutely aware that my mother would want me to say one thing, someone else may want me to say another, and then there was my own voice screaming in silence but never feeling heard.

My one place of peace was the church I had been attending since I was around thirteen years old. As a family we were raised without any particular core beliefs. My mother said she had wanted us to choose what we wanted to believe in once we were older. I had been a girl guide and I just one day asked the leader if I could go to church with her. I remember I loved how nobody shouted and argued with one another at the church; that was what appealed to me the most of all when I first went, because it was such a new experience for me. I continued going to that church into my late twenties and I am not sure to this day how I would have got by without some of the people there and the faith I had. What I often found very difficult about church was feeling like I never quite fitted in; many of the families seemed to be 'perfect' from the outside looking in and I felt so different from most of them. I guess the problem has always been within me; I'm not sure. I just never felt I fully belonged in that group of people, even though I know I was much loved. Sometimes I would walk home from church with tears streaming down my face, because I was going back to the emotional frost that awaited me at home and the contrast was so great. Also that feeling of not quite belonging anywhere was very painful. On reflection I was a much damaged young person to manage and I think the church did the best they could. I still have a lot of affection for many of the people over the years from the church, and some I will never forget. One of my earliest memories of faith is one evening when I was much younger: I had been having nightmares and I felt scared. I remember Charlie came and placed a wooden cross on my wall above my bed. I didn't really understand what that cross meant other than it brought me comfort at that moment in time.

My real family had all but kind of disowned me, having been told various versions of the truth. I remember when we were all gathered in a room together so that the social worker could explain what had happened. It was the first time since the disclosure that I found myself shut in a room with Joe. It was in fact Joe's social worker taking this session, and after she announced that Joe and I had been having a 'relationship'…yes, she used the word 'relationship'…I left that room and that house as fast as my legs could carry me. I could not believe how she had described my eight years of torment. I will never understand why she chose that word of all the words she could have used. For sometime afterwards my siblings were pretty hostile towards me. One of the saddest days was when my sister was walking up the street on the opposite side of the road and she totally ignored me. To this day I have not had a significant conversation with my siblings about the real truth, about what they know and do not know.

All of this took place in my exam years at school. In the year when you should be planning your future. Thinking about what you want to move onto doing when you leave school. My head teacher was keen for me to stay on at school into the sixth form, so I had the support. But I couldn't wait to finish school; I was literally counting down the days. That school held so many painful reminders for me of what I was going through. My mind was everywhere; at fifteen my life to me felt like it was finished. If I didn't have my family then to me I had nothing. Some of the time I should have spent revising for my exams, I could be found in the library looking up books on child abuse. Reading about other people's experiences helped me to try to begin to grasp my own situation. Somehow I passed most of my exams and I got the grades I needed to go on and do what I wanted to at college. But for many years after every summertime I felt regret and upset that I didn't do better in my exams. It is only in recent years that I have decided to give myself a break and realise that I did the best I could given the circumstances at the time. However, I can't help but sometimes wonder where I would be, what I would be today had I not been abused as a child. I know other survivors who ponder that very same question too…it's one that will never be answered. We just have to press on and make the best of where we are at now.

I lived with my foster family for six months; just before Christmas that same year the decision was made that I would be able to return home. I was to return under the watchful care of my mother and a rule was set down that Joe was not allowed to be upstairs when I was without someone else being there too. I remember my foster mum driving me home with my things, and she seemed a little hesitant about me returning. Christmas came and suddenly I was expected to sit at the dinner table with Joe and act like 'normal', which is what everyone had been doing since I came back. I thought that I was going stir-crazy at times because I had all these thoughts and feelings whizzing around inside me. It felt good to be back with my familiar surroundings but it also felt strained and a bit strange. My sister was clearly not that impressed that I was back at home. Yet everyone around me seemed to be managing and so I thought it was me who had the problem. One day I was standing at the kitchen sink washing up and the washing machine was to the right-hand side of me. The machine went onto a spin cycle and I nearly jumped out of my skin as it lightly bumped into the side of me; for a moment I thought it was Joe. Very soon after Christmas I was watching television upstairs on my parents' bed when Joe entered the room. He walked over to the bed and placed his hand on me; I knew what would come next. I shot up off that bed so fast and left him in the room alone. I was never again going to be his rag doll to be picked up and abused in that way. I just could not believe that after everything that had happened in those last six months, he would try to abuse me yet again. All the heartache, misery, meetings, and police intervention…what had it meant to him that he came and placed his hand on me once more? Did he really think that I was going to continue being there for him to use and abuse as he pleased? I was devastated but I knew I had to tell; I really didn't want to tell because now I knew what telling meant. Once I went back to school after the holidays I reported what had happened. This time Joe left home; he was placed in hostel-type accommodation. I got to stay at home but it also meant I was exposed to all of my mother's emotions over Joe leaving. I remember the day I asked her for a cuddle; she looked me straight in the face and told me she could not cuddle me. A short time later I went upstairs to see her sitting on Joe's bed, cuddling his shirt and crying her eyes out. Another time I was at home on the floor sobbing my heart out upstairs in the bedroom; the family were at home totally ignoring me but I assumed they couldn't hear me. However, someone from outside the family called in and they heard me crying and came up to try to calm me down. I still remember what they said: 'Come on, now, nothing can be that bad'. My mother told me that Joe was not eating or looking after himself, that he was very depressed. What was I supposed to say? Shortly after he went to stay with a family member. Some of the songs from the charts at that time are very poignant reminders of very unhappy times.

I continued to receive support from a social worker, much to the disapproval of my mother. Anyone in authority is treated with suspicion and contempt in my mother's eyes. I also continued with the counselling: both of these things stopped when I reached eighteen; suddenly I had no support. I can remember one of the last things my social worker said to me was that I had to deal with what had happened to me or it would make me ill, and she was right. I used to feel like my family was cursed almost: so many deeply upsetting events, seemingly one after another at times.

Within the year of leaving home Joe got a girlfriend and enjoyed bringing her back to my parents' house. He also got a job and seemed to be doing just fine. I left school and went to college to do a two year diploma, which I passed with Distinction. I thrived on my studies and the practical work placements kept me busy. Since my teens, I was forever moving the furniture around in the bedroom, tidying cupboards that didn't really need tidying…trying to gain a feeling of control where I felt I had none. I think I cleaned and tidied so much, because inside of myself felt such a mess and I didn't know how to fix it, that making changes in my environment went a little way to helping me feel better. Church continued to be a source of comfort for me. College was okay on the whole but sometimes the evenings at home alone in my room were a living nightmare. I was alone with my pain and my feelings; I knew no one in the house was interested or seemed bothered. Sometimes I just had to get out of those four walls and I would go walking late in the evening. This is where the minister of the church was amazing: he would come and find me with a flask of tea and talk to me. I remember I was always worried about using up all my credits. Let me explain about the credits! This was something which actually only existed in my own thinking; I used to feel like I was forever in danger of using up the goodness people showed to me. I saw it as credits and once I exhausted them then people's kindness would stop. I also had another constant need, which was to hear the same things again and again. For example, I would ask if I had used up all my credit and need the reassurance each time that I had not. Once we had talked the minister would make sure I was back home and not wandering around. What patience I think he had when I look back now; I was a very emotionally needy person. I guess part of the problem was that any good poured into me would be drained away again back at home. I remember one time after one of our conversations he showed me a postcard and asked me what it was. I said 'The man in the picture is screaming'…it was 'The Scream' by Edvard Munch. I had never seen the painting before, but, oh, how I could relate to it at that moment in time. I was given the postcard and I still have it today. Several years later I made my own version of 'The Scream' with clay. My mother hated the picture; in fact she hated anything that could remind her of the pain in our lives. Whilst I needed things to relate to because otherwise I felt like I was going stir-crazy, my mother was the opposite; she wanted things as 'normal' as possible. That is why I felt so totally desolate at home; nobody was being real.

At some point I began self-harming as a way to release some of the chaos inside of myself. It was like undoing the pressure valve and releasing some of the pressure. At its worst I would have fifteen plus cuts on my arms at a time. Often I had bruised or damaged knuckles too, where I would punch a wall or the window sill in my bedroom. I beat myself up a lot and yet I would never dream of hurting someone else. Sometimes I needed to exchange the emotional pain inside for physical pain. The physical pain felt easier to take and at the time of cutting I couldn't feel it. When I was calm afterwards then I would begin to feel the sting. In a rage of temper I would break a glass and then sometimes use the broken pieces to cut with. Even now if I break a glass accidentally and I'm not feeling so strong I would have to be disciplined about disposing of the broken pieces. Sometimes doing the cleaning up afterwards was soothing in itself. Self-harming is not something I would ever encourage anyone to do. It is a coping tool but as I learnt later on not a healthy one. It did become almost habitual too and it was very difficult to learn healthier coping techniques later on. I would love to be able to tell you that I never self-harm anymore but that would not be honest of me. I do still get the urge to harm when life feels overloaded and too much for me. I can usually resist and use other ways of managing. I give into it a few times in a year, which is big progress from the girl who sometimes slept with a razor by her bed. Knowing the razor was right there if I couldn't manage without it anymore used to be a comfort to me. I would often carry a razor in my bag too when I was out for that same reason; it was like a strange comfort blanket. Often that was enough and I didn't actually need to use it for harm. Another aspect of the self-harming was sometimes to punish myself, to hurt myself because I felt I had hurt others. For a long time I felt very responsible for the deep upset my disclosure had caused within the family. I hated the pain I saw etched on my mother's face, or the anger. I felt I deserved to be punished and I liked seeing myself physically hurt. I never cared about being hurt; I never felt I was important enough to worry about in that sense. In fact up until very recently I have only just begun to challenge that thought if it comes up, that it does matter and that I should mind if I am hurt.

Kate Swift

Tempted

Beautiful shiny, sleek metal
All perfectly formed and neat.
All clean and new.
Jet black screaming,
Stinging bitter pain.
Mixed with grey and blue.
Tears and heartache.
Then red, my favourite colour.
Then relief for the pain.
Then release.

~

I would get suicidal thoughts too and buy headache tablets, a box in every shop I went to…I just wanted the emotional pain to go away. At times I did feel like my family wouldn't care if I was dead, which isn't true, but it was how I felt at that time. I can remember thinking that if I was dead on the floor they would just step over me and carry on. What a dreadful thing for me to think and say but, again, that is how I felt. Shortly after my disclosure I began to write down my thoughts and feelings; often these took the form of poetry. I think writing is a very cathartic tool. You can write whatever you want and the piece of paper is not going to answer you back, challenge or contradict you. Sometimes I felt the need to rip up what I had written and other times I kept things. I don't know how I would have got through without my writing. In a house of silence it was my voice and my friend. I used to hide my writing everywhere; I even gave Sophie some to look after for me and the minister from church. In fact it was on writing this book that I revisited some of that writing. Even back then I can remember thinking I wanted to share my poems one day with other survivors of childhood abuse. I wanted them to not feel as alone as I did. I always felt if it could one day be used for good then that was what I wanted to do with it. The books I read on abuse I had to hide also in my room as my mother would not have approved of them at all. I didn't have a computer at home growing up: now there is a lot of good online support and resources so readily available, but back then I felt like the only person in the world who was going through this living hell. It was extremely difficult to manage the inner chaos and there was a long time where I felt I would never be free of him – Joe – and of what he had done to me. I felt consumed by it; not a day went by when it didn't enter my mind at least once a day. I felt tainted, grubby, unclean on the inside of me, like I had a dirty stain that could never be washed away. This made me feel different, less of a person, from other young people around me. In one of my poems I describe it like being injected with poison; I felt like he had injected me with his poison and I was going to have to live with it forever. I felt somehow different from everyone else around me, a less worthy person, a person that needed to redeem herself somehow. Yet I had absolutely no idea how to do that, how to make myself feel like I had a worth and a purpose. I was extremely conscious that my innocence was something I could never get back. I felt like I had his invisible hand prints all over me. It is like a theft but one that is so deeply personal and physical. I guess still living at home and being back in my old bedroom was a constant reminder, even with it re-decorated. I felt extremely damaged and I was extremely damaged. Not just by what Joe had done to me but also how the disclosure had been played out with my family, and everything surrounding that too. What happened after the disclosure is as painful as what happened prior, just in different ways. When Joe visited I would shut myself away in my room until he had left again. All the family carried on as normal and I felt kind of forgotten. My mum passed it off as me being a moody teenager choosing to sulk upstairs.

My Clay Interpretation of
'The Scream'

My mother's complete refusal to face up to the situation was frustrating and in its own way damaging for me. But her outward disapproval of me seeking help and support made me feel angry. I think it is one thing to decide for yourself that you will not face up to something, but quite another to actively not want the person who was the victim to get the help they need. Relatives can have this wonderful luxury that the victim does not have…the choice to be oblivious! That makes me angry, as we would love to be able to walk away from it too but we do not have that luxury because we lived it. As painful and disturbing as the truth can be, I believe if you truly love someone, you face it for them and with them. I remember just last year a relative telling me I am fine with it all now…Am I? Oh, right, thanks for letting me know! This is quite a common reaction from family, or the other reaction survivors often get is family telling them to 'forget it and move on'. Sometimes I think this is said out of a lack of understanding and the relative finding it hard to watch the person's pain. Other times I think it is said without care or feeling for the survivor…more of a selfish statement which is about that person not wanting to have to deal with the fallout or face it themselves; therefore, if the survivor quits talking about it they can live in ignorant bliss. I would urge survivors to do what they need to do in order to find peace with the past, and to not let outside pressure stop you from getting the help you need. As much as my mother protested about me seeing a social worker or a counsellor, I continued with my support; I sure needed it. Having said that, I know other survivors who have had the total opposite reaction to a disclosure of abuse by their family and that is so good and encouraging to hear. For me my family reaction was the complete opposite of what needs to happen. That is why I had to decide that I was not going to allow their behaviour to stop me from healing and from doing what I needed to heal. One day after I had been back home for a few months I remember finding a note on my pillow which read 'It is good to have my daughter back'. I can only think my mother meant this in a positive light and maybe our relationship was calmer, which prompted her to write the note. For me that note was like a kick in the teeth as I remember thinking to myself with great sadness that I had not gone anywhere; I was always there. I was always her daughter; I didn't feel like I had at any point ceased being her daughter but she obviously felt I had. It is over fifteen years now since I disclosed the abuse, and for all this time my family have carried on regardless. Never once have any of them asked me how I think or feel about what happened. Joe is treated as 'normally' as he always was and every year my mother manages to remind me of his forthcoming birthday. Why does she do that?! Does she hope that one year I will send a card? Or is she just THAT oblivious, surely not?! Thankfully I only actually see Joe a handful of times a year, the usual events such as Christmas and Mother's Day etc. It is easier to be prepared and know that I probably will see him rather than if it happens unexpectedly. On the actual day I just follow how I am feeling. If I am not feeling particularly strong that day I remove myself from the situation. Other times I immerse myself in something and we don't stay in the same room. What does everyone else do...? They carry on as if everything is just dandy!

Who are you?
You grew up in the same house as me.
Same mum and dad, same family.
You love the people that I do.
But tell me something...Who are you?

~

I did receive some loving attention after returning home but this was not from family. This was in fact from a man who was in his mid-forties...I was a school girl. He would sometimes come and meet me from school and walk me home. I liked feeling loved and cared about. I saw him as a kind of 'boyfriend' figure as that felt most appropriate to me. In time I thought I was in love with him; now I know that I of course wasn't. I was just soaking up his affection like a sponge because at that point I couldn't have felt more unpopular at home if I tried. It has taken me some time to not feel embarrassed and ashamed about it. Now I see it for what I believe it was, a grown adult having an inappropriate relationship with a teenage girl, a very vulnerable teenage girl. After all he had a daughter the very same age as me. He would call me 'Liebling', which is the German word for 'Darling'. Thank goodness we never slept together; I never had any desire to be physical with him: for me I just wanted someone to make me feel like I was worth something. I do remember very clearly the morning when I called in to see him before school: I made him a cup of tea and he was dressed only in his underwear; I was dressed in my school uniform. He told me that if I wanted to sleep with him that it would be okay because he would be careful and not get me pregnant. But as I said I had no desire to be physical in that way; I was still reeling from all that had happened to me. He had a drink problem and went on to have a long and physically abusive relationship with my sister.

At eighteen I had just finished my two year Diploma and went into my first job. I was employed as a children's nanny. I suddenly found myself feeling extremely lonely and quite isolated. I had gone from the college environment to a private house with small children. I didn't have the confidence to join social groups such as playgroups and mothers meetings when I started. Later on, as time went on and for the good of the children, I did go to social activities. That first year after college was very difficult as I found myself slipping into a major depression. I missed the busy college routine; studying kept my mind occupied. I also missed the company of other adults; suddenly I was for the most part in a big house alone with a young baby. I remained in my job but went part time. Being busy was how I functioned, but the rest of the time felt like 'doing the hours'. I used to sit in the park for hours just watching the world go by and I can remember I used to wonder to myself how they could do that…how they could just go about their day so seemingly effortlessly. I had my first course of anti-depressants at eighteen for a period of six months and they did help me a lot. The problem was I had not yet truly faced the demons of my childhood. The counselling I had done so far was more about managing day to day and airing the tensions of home life. I did not feel ready or able to delve any deeper than that. But until I did my life was not going to truly progress. One day I was walking along the river and I saw this old, half sunken boat which was covered in mud. It looked completely used up, worn out, no longer fit for any purpose. It looked abandoned; it looked like something that didn't have anything about it that would make it desirable to people anymore. I took a photograph of it because in the grip of depression that was exactly how I felt about myself. You lose all sense of purpose: just doing the day to day basics can feel like a mountain to climb. What I didn't see then which I can now is that I could be restored back to feeling like a worthwhile person with every reason for living my life. The problem was I felt what Joe had done to me defined who I was now as a person…I had to work hard to redefine myself.

Kate Swift

'The Boat'

One thing I quickly learnt, which seems ridiculous for my chosen profession in childcare and education…was that a crying child affected me quite deeply. Nobody of course likes to see or hear a child crying, but for me I needed to be able to 'fix' it fast and sometimes a hungry or tired baby is not easily soothed. I found that difficult inwardly; the need to rescue would rise to the surface. Part of it was being reminded of my own cries which had sometimes been left to me to soothe. Often when I put the baby down for a nap in the nursery I would sit in the big wicker chair and read a book or watch her sleep. I guess that is when the sheer innocence of childhood began to hit me and I was aware and deeply upset at times about my own lack of being nurtured and protected as a child myself. I remember one day I was doing some tidying and I picked up the toddler's shoes; then I stopped. I stood and looked at this tiny pair of shoes in my hands and I was suddenly awash with tears. Those shoes were again another reminder that I had once been that small, that innocent, that much in need of so much and totally reliant on the adults in my world. When faced with the trauma of dealing with the disclosure I think I really forgot that I was a child. My mood could change like the flick of a switch from being okay to crying my eyes out. You have to deal with so much that is not of a child's world that it kind of leaves you behind. Yet every day I was right back in a 'normal' family setting, seeing how the parents interacted so wonderfully with their own children, seeing how loved and nurtured they were. It didn't affect my work as I stayed with the family right through until the baby began full-time school. It just opened my eyes to perhaps what could have been and in lots of ways should have been. One of my proudest moments of my nanny days was receiving a handmade 'Nanny Day' card from the children. It was just after Mother's Day and apparently the children wanted me to have a card too. I have kept the pictures, sewing, cards and other trinkets from those years.

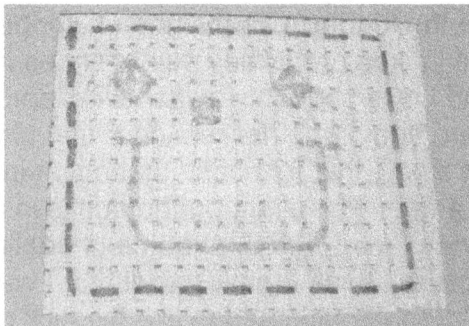

Nanny

Nanny is coming soon; she will take good care of you.

She will be your special friend until mummy and daddy's work is through.

Nanny will sing, draw, colour and play your favourite games.

She will cool you in the summer and keep you dry when it rains.

Nanny will learn all about your favourite things.

Like a shiny racing car or a pretty doll that sings.

Nanny will fill your tummies with food that makes you smile.

She will be all you need her to be each day for just a while.

Nobody's Rag Doll

She will make you laugh, make you happy.

Helping to mould you into the adult you will one day
be.

Storytelling of places far and wide.

Nanny will capture your imagination, making you
feel warm inside.

When nanny is helping others she will have her
memories.

When nanny is helping others – you will have the
poem to remember me.

~

My writing remained my main outlet for releasing
my thoughts and feelings. I could say anything I
wanted to on a piece of paper and that was very
healing. Nighttimes were the hardest and the
loneliest. Many nights were spent in my room alone
with the memories. Although Joe was no longer
living at home I would usually lock myself in my
room; I had a proper key lock fitted to my bedroom
door. I slept really badly, often not getting to sleep
until dawn was breaking. I would sit by the window
staring out into the night trying to escape my inner
self. Sometimes I found the cold night air really
refreshing; it reminded me I was indeed alive. Joe
visited home and always had an air of arrogance
about him. To me he seemed to be doing just fine,

whilst I felt like I was constantly trying not to drown. He landed a good job with a very respectable company. He had his girlfriend who was already expecting their first child; his life from the outside looking in seemed to be unblemished and that to me felt so unjust. I wondered back then as I do sometimes now: did he think about what he had done – did it keep him awake at night? To be honest I hoped that it did because to see him so smug and seemingly without a care was difficult.

It was around this same time that I had my first boyfriend. At first he seemed lovely, kind and thoughtful. He was all of those things until he drank, and what I didn't know when we began seeing each other was that he had a drink problem. He was my first love and I stayed with him much longer than I should have stayed. We were both needy in different ways: we both had our damage; we both felt the need for each other in our lives. It was some time before I told him what had happened to me in terms of the sexual abuse. I did not go into many details – just enough so that, I hoped, he would understand me a bit better. Drinking turned him into a different person; he became very aggressive verbally and, at times, physically too. Many a night I guided him safely to his bed so he could sleep it off. The other tedious, to the point of mind numbing, task was having to listen to the drunken ramblings until he did finally fall asleep. I was never gladder than when I heard his snoring and the relief would sweep over me. Sometimes people would telephone me from his favourite drinking place to inform me that he was about to get himself into a fight. I would go and fetch him and coax him out of the bar. I was very fearful of what may happen to him or what he could do to someone else when totally drunk. I used to tell him my fears but it didn't seem to register with him; he really was like two different people...the drunk and the sober nice guy. I remember one night he even tried to fight his own shadow. I worried about his well-being and other people's. When it was good it was fine but when it was bad it was really the pits. In my naivety I truly believed my love would be enough to make him a better person. All my love did in reality was facilitate his ugly behaviour and addiction to the alcohol. I took the ranting and the abuse, I cleaned up the mess, and I forgave him over and over...thus, I was facilitating his behaviour. I know that now but at the time I thought it would be okay. Sometimes after a violent outburst the following morning he would say sorry and tell me he was leaving. You would think I would be helping him to pack but I was actually begging him to stay with me. I was convinced that I needed him and that without him I didn't really have anything. This was a man who had previously stamped on my arm in his working boots, thrown a hardback book at my spine and more than once had his hands around my throat. He would also tell me to go and cut myself or to take an overdose. Of everything that he did one of the worst was when he used his knowledge of my past to be extremely cruel...he would call me 'brother lover'. I know he sounds like a really horrible person, and yet when he was sober he was totally different. However, that's no excuse for his behaviour and I wish I had been stronger and come to my senses sooner. But he was and always will be my first love even though I know he is not healthy for me. I am sure I was no easy person to be in a relationship with either. All of my own demons and insecurities were still very much a part of my everyday life...but then these were what allowed him to behave how he did. There is no excuse for domestic violence; it is never acceptable, be it a man hitting a woman or vice versa...men get hurt too. The break finally came after a particularly frightening incident late one evening after yet another of his heavy drinking sessions. He came home from the pub after closing time and was once again extremely drunk. I was in the bedroom and he came in and shut the door behind him. He then leant up against the door and told me I needed to telephone the police because he was going to kill me. There was no telephone in the bedroom – the panic rose inside of me like furious flames. I walked towards the door and he grabbed me by the throat. We struggled, and because he was so drunk he lost his footing and stumbled. This was my moment to run out the door...I ran down the stairs and telephoned my mother to come home, but before I could speak he was behind me pulling out the cord from the wall. I then ran out into the street in my bare feet. My mother came down the road; I was fairly hysterical by this point. Just then a police car drove down and pulled up outside. A neighbour had telephoned them as they had heard his threats to kill. My mother as always made light of the situation and I didn't get the opportunity to speak. It was after that incident that I finally came to my senses and realised enough was enough. I might have loved this person but he was no good for me, and I made the break. Sometimes you have to listen to your head even when your heart is screaming something else at you. He was my first sexual partner and it was extremely difficult for me. I have to say he was very patient and waited months before I could even bring myself to kiss him fully. When we did finally sleep together I would turn away afterwards and cry. I can't help but think about my own parents' relationship as I write this chapter. The phrase history repeating itself comes to my mind somewhat as I think back to those drunken rages of my father all those years before. I was fortunate to have church folk stick by me throughout this relationship even though they openly and, quite rightly, disapproved of it. I would love to be able to say that was my only bad relationship but I had another: did I really need a reminder? I guess I must have done, although the next one was a very different kind of bad. It is difficult to not feel like I am bringing a lot of baggage to any relationship because I feel like I am. Although, as time goes on I think I bring less baggage forward with me. I certainly would never be in another abusive relationship; I am a different person today as I retell my past. I know that I deserve better and that violence is never acceptable. My sister has also had several very abusive relationships. The worrying thing is I don't think she has enough sense of self to say no to another one.

My feelings of love faded and died.
When you got drunk, hit me and lied.
I thought you were all I needed to feel okay.

Kate Swift

I thought I could love you enough to make
Your alcoholism go away.
I thought it was all about me getting it wrong,
making you drink.
But now I realise that is what you wanted me to
think.
To feel sorry for you, to forgive and forgive.
When do I get my life to live?

~

You are draining the life out of me.
Why won't you just let me go free?
Why do you want to hurt me so bad?
What do I do that makes you so mad?
I loved you with all the love I had to give.
Now I am begging, pleading and screaming
That you will take your hands from my throat.
That you will let me get out of the door.
That you will let me live.

~

Thanks for telling me I'm nothing but I knew that
already.
Don't think that I have any grand ideas of illusions
about me.
I don't know why you're so hellbent on bringing me
down.
You don't know how many times I have hit the
ground.
I know what I am; I live with me every day.
Maybe it's from yourself that you want to get away.

~

A part of me remembers
A loud unexpected noise.
The slamming of a door,

Nobody's Rag Doll

The raised voice of a drunk.
& my body remembers.
I freeze and then panic rises.
I suddenly feel so small.
Small and terrified.
My mind goes into overdrive.
The noise is not here.
The threat is not here.
The screaming is not here.
I am safe from everything I heard.
It is just that part of me remembers,
Remembers what you did.
Remembers the thud of your fist.
Remembers the breaking of glass.
Remembers the hand on my throat.
Remembers the slap across my face.
Remembers the tone of your voice.
Remembers the look in your eyes.
Then silence.
I can breathe a little easier again.
Until the next time…
A part of me remembers.

~

Always a reason…

It was the middle of winter and the sky was as
black as the bruises on her body.
But she said…'He loves me and he said he will get
help soon; you'll see'.

The spring came and the blossom burst open like
her lip did when he punched her face.

Kate Swift

But she said…'He loves me and soon we will live happily and far away from this place'.

The days got lighter but there was no summer in her home, as he battered her each day.
But she said…'He loves me and he really doesn't mean to react in this way'.

Autumn came and the leaves began to fade and die, just like her spirit fading and dying.
But she said…'He loves me and he really is sorry; he hates to see me crying'.

It was the middle of winter and the sky was as black as the hearse where her coffin lay.
A little child looked up with tears running down his face and said, 'Why did my mummy go away?'

~

Wish I could share with you, implant in you the gift…
The gift of insight I gained whilst getting battered.
When holding onto him and his love seemed to be all that mattered.
Wish I could show you how yours will not change in the way you think, dream, hope he will.
So you didn't have to suffer whilst waiting for your fairytale to be become real.
Wish I could prove to you how strong you really are.
Before he drains the very lifeblood out of you, pushes you too far.

Wish I could show you what I learnt whilst I thought
I was in love with him and he with me.
How you are enslaved yet you think if you stick with
him you will both one day be free.
Wish I could show you what love really is.
A gentle hug, a helping hand, a soothing kiss.
Wish I could show you what I failed to see when I
was standing where you are today.
Please don't take abuse…not for one more day.

~

In between all of this happening I made a visit to
see a doctor. I told them I was feeling extremely
down and struggling a lot. The doctor referred me
for some brief intervention counselling. During
these sessions I talked about my parents and my
life as it was at that point of time. I told her about
the abuse but only as a point in my 'history' – very
matter of fact and with little emotion. It was shortly
after this she shocked me by telling me that my
need for counselling was not about the things I had
discussed. It was the massive thing I had not talked
about with her, which was the abuse. I truly was
shocked, I guess at that stage I had made the
decision that I was 'okay' with it. I agreed for her to
refer me on for further assessment and treatment. I
was also on another course of antidepressants;
they were another thing my mother didn't agree
with! I know many people do not like the idea of
taking tablets, in particular antidepressants. I
believe they can provide the necessary scaffolding
(support) whilst you work on the issues actively with
a counsellor or whoever it may be. I'm not sure that

I could have made it through some of the stages without them. Attitudes towards mental health have moved on immensely, but we still have a way to go in how these things are viewed. I can remember going through a stage of resenting the tablets: I used to think 'Why do I need to take a tablet to make me feel okay when others just are okay without the aid of anything?' Depression is an illness in the same way as other illnesses and we must look on it in a similar way.

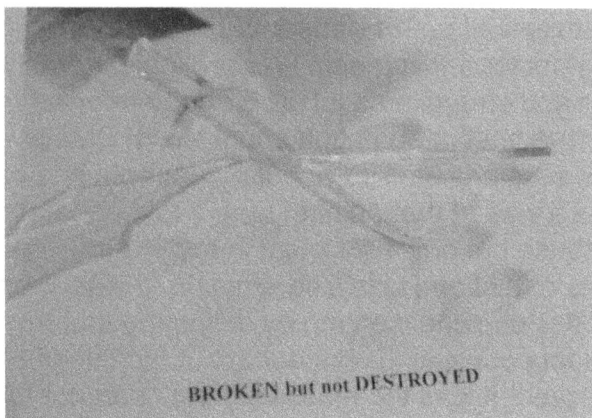

BROKEN but not DESTROYED

My favourite job to date was my time spent in a local school. I worked there in the Early Years department for several years. I can remember feeling for the first time that everything was going well, that I was happy and enjoying my life. Whilst that is true, I was also working like crazy. I would go into work early and stay at work long after I was due to finish. I would then be bringing work home with me to take me through the evening until I could get up the following morning and do it all over again. By this time I was settled with weekly sessions seeing a psychologist and keeping myself very busy! Those early months in my psychology sessions were filled with silences. It took a long time to feel comfortable and able to begin to open up. Also, to take myself back in my mind, to dare to open up the door on all that was horrible about my past, was difficult. At that point I didn't understand the necessity of having to work through my childhood to find some sense of peace to go forwards. I believe there are no quick fixes to healing this kind of damage; it takes time and as much as we wish we could make it go quicker we need to go through the process, just as a vehicle has to journey through the tunnel to come out the other end into the light. If you commit to your therapy you should see results but these may not be apparent to you for some time. Many survivors tell me they couldn't possibly talk about what happened to them, but for as long as you live with that door firmly closed up tight other than inside of your own head, it still has power over you to make you fear what is there. As wretched as it is, if we can find it within ourselves to stare it in the face, it begins to lose its power over us. As I write this book now, looking back I can say that for all the pain and discomfort I have gone through with therapy…I have gained a better understanding…some closure…knowledge…confidence…self-empowerment…being able to say and believe (after loads of therapy) that the abuse was not my fault. It has given me time to think…space to think…to evaluate and re-evaluate…to challenge or strengthen my thinking on certain things. It has done such a lot for me and I really don't know where I would be now without it. That is why I will be ever thankful to my psychologist Chris and why I dedicated my first book 'This Tangled Web' to him. I think such a lot can be gained from therapy. I liked my psychologist Chris; he seemed genuinely very interested and concerned about me. Early on I began to bring him my writings from home, and these, I guess, were a good picture of what was going on for me. Chris often commented that I should think about getting them published in the future. Bringing in writing was also a very safe and relatively easy way to share some of the worst of my experiences. Handing over some poems was nothing compared to if I had to sit and vocalise the content. Work went really well for the first few years and I seemed to please my colleagues (people pleasing!). The sessions with Chris continued week on week; the harder the sessions, the harder I worked outside of them to avoid thinking and feeling about them. Sometimes I promised myself a small treat after a session as a kind of reward to myself for getting through it. This didn't have to cost money, although sometimes I bought myself some flowers. It could be painting your nails, going for a lovely walk, having a bubble bath…anything that gives you some pleasure. My coping mechanism of keeping extremely busy at work and at home served me fairly well for quite some time, but what I didn't bargain on was me grinding to a complete stop.

In therapy the one thing I found hard to express was anger. I was and still am afraid of anger. I have seen it spill over and do so much damage. But I know that anger conveyed in a measured way can be healthy. Here is a piece of writing I did in my mid-twenties…

Feeling ANGRY this morning but more than anger I'm getting tears and that too is making me angry, because I'm tired of tears. I am in such a state at the thought of therapy this afternoon. We are getting in deep now and I know I need to go there and I know (hope) it will all be worth it but OUCH. Didn't sleep much last night – was feeling really anxious, which was making me really nauseous… aaaaaaaaaaaahhhhhhhhhhhh! I'm angry with HIM…how dare he have done this to me. How dare I be going through all of this hell whilst HE has a life? How dare I be in this state more than 10 years after my abuse stopped…how dare I still be paying this damn cost…I want HIM to suffer today…I want HIM to feel ripped and torn inside and raw and not be able to sleep, and jump at the slightest noise and push everyone away because it feels safer, and then to feel the aloneness. I am struggling to type because my hands are real shaky. CAN'T DO THIS, CAN'T CAN'T CAN'T…I HATE HIM, I HATE HIM, I HATE HIM, I HATE HIM, I HATE HIM, I HATE HIM…I'M SORRY but I HATE HIM and I hate these feelings and having to go through all of these emotions; I just want to be 'normal'; I was born a 'normal' baby. I CANT DO ALL THIS ANYMORE.

Kate Swift

This is a letter I wrote to – HIM – I wrote it just to vent how I was feeling at the time; it was not something I ever sent. It gives you an idea of how I was feeling about things at that time…

I spent my late teens and early 20's feeling like you had stolen my childhood innocence and so many possibilities away from me growing up…but the older I get the more I'm realising that you stole a whole lot more from me than I even realised before, such as my ability to form a strong and meaningful relationship…my ability to be intimate with someone I love…and, worst of all, no matter how old I get…when I'm elderly…when I'm dying…I will now always have been 'an abused person'…even when I have happy times, you seem to find a way to creep in there at some point in some way, whether it's a nightmare, a memory, a smell, something on TV, etc. I know that I can live happily but I also know that you will always have abused me and that twists deep inside me…knowing I can't outgrow or outlive what you did. Like when you put dirty linen through the wash and make it lovely and new again…I wish in some way I could do that too…that I could go through some kind of cleansing and forever remove what you did. Even when I feel okay and I feel it doesn't matter…it does matter because what you did shapes a lot of what I do…how I feel about myself, my inability to be intimate with someone I choose, my overprotective nature with children and all that kind of thing. Oh, don't get me wrong: I'm not just going to blame you for everything; I can own my own failures. Furthermore, you go on to have a successful career and beautiful children…children that I never see, whom I wrap gifts for and leave with a mutual relative; who I try to guess what they would like because I don't see them to know what they are into as they grow older each year, and when another relative talks about them like when she said she was taking them out for the day it really hurts. I'd like to get all the self-help books off my shelf and shove them in your face…I'd like to lock you in a room with my therapist so he can tell you just the kind of damage you did. I've always said I never wish you any harm because I hate violence, but in some way – even though I feel bad for saying this – but in some way I'd like to see you suffer…The crazy thing is I probably wouldn't enjoy it anyway because I am me. How can you steal a little girl's childhood and then go on to live your seemingly successful life? How can a mother look at her abused daughter with bitterness and say 'Did you lay back and think of England'…? Sometimes I think I have untangled the web you wove within me…other times like right now I feel so tangled up in it like it's pressing against my skin and I cannot move. One thing is for sure, though: I will not stay held captive by what you did; I will fight to the death to be rid of your filthy, rotten, dirty shame.

My job in the school meant I travelled passed the Social Services department that I had attended for my own case conferences and meetings. I found it an unpleasant reminder of a very unhappy time, having to go past it five days a week. So I made the decision to try to lay that part of my past to rest. I applied to be able to go back and read through my file. It was not straightforward obtaining the permission to do so, but I was stubborn and determined! Eventually, when I was getting nowhere fast, I contacted the Director of Social Services and then things moved quickly and I was able to go and look through my file. It was strange walking back through those doors; the department looked exactly the same as it had when I was fifteen; only now I was in my late twenties. I ended up going back a second time as my file was like a volume of a telephone directory! The duty social worker who greeted me on my second visit said a very lovely thing to me when I was leaving. She said I seemed to be a very different person from the one she had read about in my file, that I had come a long way. Indeed I had come a distance but nowhere near far enough. It was still good to know I had picked myself up from those chaotic teenage years and I had survived thus far.

One bright sunny morning I was in work early as was usual for me. I began setting up the classroom but I also began to cry. The problem came when I tried to calm myself and stop crying…I couldn't manage it. My colleague and, now, my dear friend in the classroom next door came through and gently suggested that I needed to go home. This was duly arranged and I went home for the day; the following morning the exact same thing happened and I was told to go and see my doctor. Looking back now I guess I was extremely tired, doing my therapy and coping with home life, which was always up and down. I never slept very well: I was usually asleep late and awake early. I remember a

On the work front I was not able to remain well enough – long enough to return to work. My job was kept open for me for quite some time before I was made redundant on health grounds. It is not how I would have chosen to end a job that I loved doing but for my own sake it had to be that way. I have maintained contact with two of my work colleagues and both are very dear friends to me. In therapy we worked on many different elements of what had happened. One of the most liberating was learning and understanding how dysfunctional families operate, learning how to take myself out of the mind games people can play. The second most liberating thing was accepting that my parents were not perfect, in particular my mum: she had not been the best mum she could have been. It was hard at first to hear her criticised and I would often try to defend her actions or lack of action. Over time I could see that whilst she loved me and felt she did her best for me, her best was not enough. I took her off the pedestal I had placed her on when I was a very small child. This freed me up to go and seek the approval or whatever it was I needed emotionally from other much healthier sources. I am often asked now how can I continue to have a relationship with a parent who failed me so badly. But the truth is this…as a mum she messed up and I don't try to defend that anymore. However, as a person and still as my mum, I love her very dearly. I separate my childhood from the relationship that we have now. It is the only way I have found it can work. For the sake of wanting to maintain my bond and my relationship with her that is the choice I made. It is not for everybody – we are all different –

but for me I still love her dearly and want her in my life. Our relationship is much more on equal footing now that I am an independent adult and we know where the boundaries are. It doesn't mean that I never get sad and wish for it to be different, because at times I have. I wrote a poem about this called 'The Empty Well'; I learnt to see her as an empty well, me with my bucket going every day to draw some water. Every day coming away feeling emotionally thirsty, no water in that well for me. Once you realise the source is for whatever reason empty or not going to give you what you need, you are freed up to go elsewhere and be nourished. I spent a long time waiting and hoping for the perfect family: I didn't get perfect – it is not a realistic goal – and I moved on with what I do have. If I never accepted those truths I would still be trying to draw water from the empty well and coming away feeling totally despondent. It does not mean, either, that how she behaved over those years no longer matters and I have just forgotten it: it can't be erased or undone. The damage of her rejection and behaviour following the abuse disclosure was deeply wounding but what do I gain from being hateful? I cannot see that I gain anything; it's not that I don't feel anger about it because I do. I cannot make peace with the rejection and my mum has never attempted to address the issue. Her favourite line is 'I clothed and fed you, didn't I!' and, yes, she did; that is correct…but why she thinks that is all she needed to do as a mother to six children is somewhat beyond me. That is where I think possibly that her own lack of mothering comes into play. Again, that is not an excuse – it is a reason – but I strongly feel you owe it to your own children to mend anything that is within your control to mend. Wherever possible I believe your own children should not suffer the ill-effects of your own childhood, because as an adult you have the ability to heal and to change the future. What my mother failed to realise is that feeding and clothing the body is all very necessary for physical survival but feeding and clothing your child's soul is equally as vital. I always remember being struck by something my friend Jane did as a mother with her daughter. Every night when her daughter was going to bed, Jane would sit on the end of her bed and chat with her about the day just gone by. I think that is a really lovely thing to do, and what a great opportunity to talk about all those important things. If you are reading this book and you have children, don't forget to tell them that you love them. Often we don't tell children they are loved: showing they are loved is key but to tell them too means a great deal. Love for your own child should be unconditional.

Enough?

I know that you have love for me…
But do you love me enough to set me free?
Do you love me enough to walk with me through
the fire?
Through the burning embers of his twisted and sick
desire.
Do you love me enough to stand in the centre and
feel the heat?
To hear your little girl scream and scream, yet not
retreat.
Do you love me enough to see that I actually did no
wrong?
To tell me I was caught in a nightmare to which I
did not belong.
I know that you love me…but do you love me
enough?

~

Before I reached that understanding many things
happened which also changed and re-shaped mine
and my mother's relationship. Our relationship hit a
rock bottom point when I was at home all day. I was
with my second boyfriend who again I thought was
'perfect'. We had met in a church, well inside the
church bookshop! He said he needed someone to
talk to about his problems; the staff were busy and
so I volunteered to listen to him. We sat in the
church and I listened for quite some time. Following
on from this he contacted my local church and
asked if we could meet again; he arrived with
flowers and it went from there. I quite quickly

decided this was the man I was going to marry and have children with. I was very much in love and he seemed like the perfect gentleman. He brought me flowers and took me out for meals, all those usual things. He promised to protect me and take care of me. The church were impressed by him too and everyone seemed to like him. He talked about engagement rings and our future together. He wasn't terribly interested in being physical with me, which suited me very well! It was whilst I was with him that I left home. It was something I should have done a lot sooner but one day things came to a head for me and I decided to go. Many people will wonder why on earth I had not left home a lot sooner than this but I was waiting…waiting for the 'perfect family'. I lived in hope that someday I would have the kind of family I had always wanted. Professionals and others around me had felt I should leave home a long time before I did, but I just couldn't see what I would have if I didn't have my family. As dysfunctional and chaotic as they were they were my family and they meant a great deal to me. For me, moving out of the family home was admitting that I would never have the family I wanted and that was painful; in fact I feel a twinge of pain as I write about it now. But things at home were really difficult and I left in a fit of anger one day, and then there was no going back: I'd finally made the break. Part of me had wanted to go and part of me had wanted the fairytale endings. Initially I stayed with a dear friend, and she was extremely kind to me. This could only be a short-term arrangement as she needed the room come term time, for a student. With no job, no income and severe depression, I had to report myself as homeless at the beginning of that academic year. It was one of the lowest days of my life, sitting in the local housing department with one bag of my belongings. The rest of my things were packed up and being stored at the church... another kindness they showed to me. All of my life I had craved a loving, happy and secure home and now I was facing the complete unknown. I wanted to be a little girl again so I could put my hand inside my mum's and be wrapped up in cotton wool, but that was not an option. Sometimes in life you have to get on and rescue yourself; nobody is going to do it for you... and for me this was one of those times. I was really afraid of being put into temporary accommodation, of living with strangers, of not having control over my environment once again. But I was fortunate, depending on how you look at it (!), to be placed in a local bed and breakfast facility: at least I had a roof over my head. My time at the B&B was something of a steep learning curve. I had a very small room with a single bed, wardrobe, fridge and bedside cabinet. Still, I tried to make it nice: I bought some Carnations and cut down a fizzy drinks bottle to use as a vase. My then boyfriend was still around but our relationship was going downhill fast, and the bubble burst for me the night I discovered him smoking cocaine. I am very strongly anti-drugs and I was deeply shocked; I had absolutely no idea. I felt so stupid and naive but I was also really angry as we had next to no money to survive on, cornflakes for dinner some nights, and he had spent £50.00 on illegal drugs. When I began to challenge him about it he quickly changed from being a nice person to someone who actually once spat in my face. I have since learnt that he was someone who conned people out of money. Worst of all was that he took the time to get to know people, made friends with them and then conned them out of money. I was left wondering if anything he ever said to me in terms of how he felt for me was true; I guess in hindsight it was not. It was a means to an end as the saying goes. I remember the night I was sitting on the floor crying and he bent down and very gently kissed my tears…so tender and loving…so false and cruel.

Everyone thought you were oh so nice.
They saw a happy couple and they did not see the price.
The conversations when we were on our own.
We were seen as 'two' but I felt so betrayed and so alone.
You spoke at first with words so beautiful, full of promise.
You placed on my tears a silent tender kiss.
But none of it was true; none of it was real.
It was all for what you wanted, all to get your deal.
You smiled in public, screamed at me at night.
You talked like a charmer, fooled the world we were alright.
You held my hand in the street, chained my soul with your lies.
You told me you wanted marriage and children; it was all a disguise.

'Great bloke': that is what people around us said.
All the time my hopes lay dying and dead.
You never laid a finger on me yet you beat me up inside.
Close in public, in private, so far and wide.
Inside of myself where no one could see.
See the mental bruises you rained down on me.
The way your angry words tore open the wounds in my mind.
The battering of every word that was twisted and unkind.
The echoes of what you said that played over and over again.
I would rather physical pain.
Sounds crazy but physical pain has a time frame to heal.
People can see it, and in seeing it to them it becomes real.
…Everyone thought you were oh so nice.

~

Life at the bed and breakfast was quite tough I found; some of the other residents were nice people and I made some friends. Others were not the kind of people I would have chosen to be sharing a house with but you don't have much choice. For someone who had always wanted the fairytale ending this for sure was not it. I had craved security all of my life but now I was in a place where I felt less secure than ever in some ways. However, there were some lighter moments. I remember one evening with much amusement when one of the other residents knocked on my door and asked if they could borrow a plate…a few minutes later they came and knocked again and asked to borrow a knife…a few minutes later…well, yes, you get the picture! The caretaker of the premises was partial to a drink and was often passed out by 3pm. The electricity would sometimes cut out early evening, and as the caretaker was by then often semi-unconscious from the drink, you had to just wait for the following morning until it was fixed. This meant an early night and a cold shower the next day. My washing would take two or three days to dry on the washing line because I washed it in the little sink in my room and wrung it out as best I could with my hands. The communal areas were not very clean and this too got me down; eventually I reported it and I was moved to a much nicer house. These are some extracts from a letter I wrote to the local authority regarding my temporary accommodation…

'On the third evening of my stay at the house the doorbell was ringing constantly. This was followed by two men banging on my window as my room is at the front of the house. I later discovered the men were owed money from someone staying in the house. This was a very frightening and unsettling experience.'

'The fridge in my room was leaking badly. I reported this to the caretaker, who told me he already knew the fridge needed replacing! The carpet around the fridge is constantly soggy and the fridge is of no use for keeping food fresh.'

'I have an en suite bathroom for which I was thankful. However, it is very damp. I have to listen to the sound of running water constantly. Sometimes it is so loud that I wake up and think it is heavy rain fall outside. The toilet was leaking when I arrived and to date has not been fixed. Due to the permanent damp the woodwork is rotting away.'

'One male resident shouts at himself all night and then sleeps all the day. I have residents asking me for food, clothing, money, washing powder: they are clearly struggling to look after themselves and need more help.'

'Last weekend I had no electricity, for all of Friday night through to the following morning. It went out again on Saturday evening and was out then until Monday.'

'On Friday the 10th of October there was a very serious incident involving drugs, a gun and a knife, yet again, a very frightening experience to be in.'

Getting moved to a different house in a different area was how I made my break from the current boyfriend: I left his things behind with no forwarding address and I moved. I felt guilty for some time afterwards, thinking about him returning that evening to find me gone and to be handed just his bag. But that was the only way I could get rid of him from my life and I wanted to be on my own. From that day to this we have never had another conversation; I have seen him in the street once. So moving accommodation brought me some new freedom. My mother and her friend helped me to move to the new house, and whilst it was a much better standard of living, it felt so far away from everything and everyone I knew. When I visited home it was pleasant enough and relationships were better. But when I returned to the bed and breakfast house I felt like I didn't have anything really much at all. One of the other residents used to knock on my door and ask to borrow money, which, although he wasn't unpleasant, I found somewhat intimidating. I tried to make it work but I became increasingly depressed. I ended up spending a short time in the mental health unit as an inpatient. This was voluntary; I wanted to escape from everything including myself. Most of the staff were okay but I hated my psychiatrist with a passion! This was a man who knew next to nothing about me, who sat in meetings making decisions about me! At one point he concluded that I was not depressed before discharging me with…anti-depressants to take. I didn't want to leave the hospital when I was discharged; I didn't feel strong enough or ready. My nurse said as much to me the night before I was due to be discharged. I remember her saying that most patients when being discharged were extremely happy to be going home and I was the total opposite. That to her she said was an indicator that I was not ready to go home. I was referred to the day hospital which I attended a few times. I was still seeing Chris for my weekly therapy sessions but progress, I guess, was delayed by my mental state at that time.

SHE...
She is broken.
She is pierced.
She is fractured.
She is torn.
She is splintered.
She is fragmented.
She is split.
She is shattered.
SHE...

~

It was not until sometime after I got well again that I realised just how ill I had become. I would go to the high street, walk around the shops but not buy anything because I would be telling myself I did not need anything. I was planning to not be around for another year. My plan was to see Christmas through – in my mixed up thinking I knew I couldn't spoil Christmas – but then after that I could go. I spent Christmas at home with the family, just as I always did, and nobody picked up on how unwell I had become. But then I was doing my best to be 'normal' and to get through it. The following piece of writing is an exact copy of what I wrote on the 23rd of December of that year. I decided to include it in this book, as I think it shows more accurately than I can describe now of how I was feeling and thinking at that exact time in my life.

Dear Life,

I have to vent some of my feelings, so strong inside of me that I don't know what to do with myself today. I really despise you today, you and your endless hours. I have drawn the curtains to shut out the light and I have covered over the clock but still you hang heavy within me. Feel SO low today and SO alone. Not that I haven't got friends who will talk to me, but how can they understand all my many thoughts of suicide. Calm, considered thoughts like suicide would be more difficult for people at this time of the year. I got the razor out to cut and then was put off when I turned over my arm and saw scars already there…red and angry. So I just held the razor in my hand for a while and the tablets beside me. I can't say its one thing that keeps drawing my thoughts to suicide, no one major issue; just don't want this life. Most of the year my main focus was a flat but now that doesn't seem like one of my answers anymore: I didn't bother to bid this last month because it feels so pointless. Part of me can see that this is my spell of 'black' thinking and I've been here before; it will pass but the rest of me feels tired and scared. I rang the ward today for help and they told me to go to A&E (Accident and Emergency) but I couldn't face all that. Never before have my feelings of suicide been so debated in my head, because probably for the first time I think I have enough tablets to do it properly, which means I have to really want it, no messing about, no half-hearted thoughts…life or death?…70 anti-depressants, 20 painkillers, 35 sleeping tablets, 30 antibiotics…is that enough?

Kate Swift

When life is so exhausting death seems inviting; it's almost like a torment. That every hour you spend living you're aware that you could be dead and that would be easier. Jane has rung a couple of times today knowing I feel low but her words and other people's words are just bouncing off the surface. Whilst they are talking about shopping or TV, my head is full of pain. How can I begin to explain that? Maybe I am just thinking too much that in a split second I could just get on with it. Do I want to be found dead in a council bed and breakfast? Strange, because I thought when it came down to it I wouldn't care about things like that but obviously I do. Selfish of me to sit here debating my life when others have theirs cruelly snatched away with no choice. I know I'm being very selfish and suicide would be very self-indulgent but I'm the one who has to live my life, nobody else. Sometimes I really want to be back in hospital because a lot of the time I feel on edge and unable to cope out here. I feel like throwing the clock against the wall because its ticking is like torment today. Why do the worst days feel so long? Would I write a suicide letter or would the act itself be like a letter to those whom it would bother? What significance my life, wherever I took myself? I thought about other ways of hurting myself today, counteracting one pain with a different kind of pain…a kettle of boiling water…but could I go through with it? I don't know. Today they are just thoughts in my head; maybe tomorrow they will be a reality or maybe I will have better thoughts. But right now tomorrow seems so far away and I feel so exhausted. Soon I can have sleep and sleep brings relief, but then there's another day ahead.

Depression is just so mentally crushing. Some of the loneliest places are rooms full of people. I felt lonely a lot and yet I didn't want anyone around me. I could have called up a friend but I didn't want to. The days felt endless and I longed for the night time as I knew the phone wouldn't ring and the door wouldn't knock. Days are like an endurance test: if you get up you just long to be able to go back to bed. I stumbled on until December 31st; the night before that I felt so low and I remember I prayed to God to make me sleep all the night because if not I couldn't make it…that night I slept really well. It didn't bring relief from how I was feeling the following day. In the morning I had an appointment with my doctor. My doctor was quite shocked at how low I was; she wanted me to go and see somebody at the hospital that same day. I was sent to the day hospital with a letter and I went. I saw my key worker and a duty psychiatrist who had never met me before. The psychiatrist asked me some questions and I had some questions for him. I wanted to know how many tablets I needed to take to make sure that I died. I really, seriously wanted to know the answer to my question. In my head my thinking was extremely black and white, very matter of fact. However, it would seem to this psychiatrist that my question was intended to seek attention or provoke a reaction. He told me if I wanted some help to stop saying such things. At that point I gave up trying to communicate anything in that room; I knew at that point that I was going home to die. Before I had even left the day hospital I knew. In the end the decision was given to me…did I want to be admitted to a ward or did I want to go home. Well, I already knew what I was doing and I told them I would go home. My dear friend Jane came and collected me and drove me home; it was a really cold wintry day. Jane came into the B&B with me but I was anxious for her to leave; she talked to me about coming to a social event later that evening for New Year's Eve. As soon as Jane had left I gathered together all the medication I had which was quite a lot; I got a large glass of water, put some music on and began to swallow the tablets. At that point all I wanted was to be out of it: the emotional pain was too much and I just did not want to do another year and another year was fast approaching. My memory after taking the tablets becomes very hazy. All I can remember is sitting on the bed and seeing my little red bike with the carousel on it that I had loved as a child…then I saw one of my relatives to say goodbye to.

HERE

I AM HERE.
I BREATHE.
I LIVE.

I AM ALIVE.
I FUNCTION.
I SURVIVE.

I AM A SOUL.
I AM A BODY.

I AM A MIND.

I TRIED TO DIE:
SUICIDE.

YET I AM HERE.
I BREATHE.
I LIVE.

~

The next time I was aware of anything was twenty-four hours later. I woke up in a hospital bed with a lady in the bed next to me. I got up and found the bathroom, looked in the mirror and saw that my face was all grazed and bruised, but I had no idea how. As I became more aware of my surroundings I learnt that I was in a heart unit. The nurse came and filled in some of the blanks for me; she told me my friend had phoned an ambulance. I had one question I wanted to know from the nurse…if I had not been found would I have died…her answer was…yes. I felt angry with Jane for calling for help. I could not, of course, say that to her at the time but I was angry. I remember thinking to myself at that point that the next attempt I would ensure would work. I just did not want to be around anymore and it took a long time for that to change. I felt totally emotionally spent; every day felt like it was to be endured. I would get up in the morning and long for bedtime. Sophie came to see me with my mum, also. My mother was deeply upset and told me I obviously didn't love her enough to have done what I had. But it wasn't about how much I did or didn't love people; it was about wanting all the pain to go away. That day the minister from church came to visit me too; I don't remember much about either visit.

Shattered like a hammer through glass.
Waiting for the thoughts to pass.
Sifting through the pieces with bleeding fingers and broken dreams.
Torn and twisted, falling apart at the seams.
My soul is limping like a wounded animal.
Broken pieces and bleeding fingers, that is all.

~

In the days that followed I had those missing twenty-four hours filled in for me. Jane said she was at home that New Year's Eve several hours after she had dropped me back to the B&B, and she had a nagging feeling that something was very wrong with me. Jane tried to call me and she also asked the minister at church to try calling me too. I can't recall any of that, even to this day. I'm told I did answer the phone at some point but I wasn't making sense and they called an ambulance. Jane called my mum and she came to the hospital and stayed with me until I was out of danger and on a ward, not that I was aware of her being there. From the heart unit I was told I would need to be transferred back to the mental health unit at the other hospital. I remember when the doctor told me I immediately said I did not want to return to the unit; I said that they didn't want or like me there. That is how I was left feeling following my first stay there. However, the doctor assured me that it would be fine and that, yes, they did want to look after me.

That night I was transported in my hospital gown, still feeling quite groggy, to the unit. After a time of being asked to wait in the television room, I was shown to my room. To my horror it was like someone already occupied the room: it was dirty; the bed was unmade; there was a dirty cup on the side, etc. I told the nurse I could not stay in that room; it belonged to someone else but she told me it was my room. I asked her for some clean sheets and she came and placed them on the chair. I was still feeling physically quite unwell and too ill to even make the bed. I took myself back down the corridor and spoke to a different nurse; thankfully he was lovely and totally got what I was saying about the room. That nurse had it cleaned and sorted ready for me. That first night I had to sleep with the door open and a nurse was right outside the door to keep a watch on me…I can tell you one thing…that nurse slept really well that night! All medication was stopped, as is procedure, I believe, following an overdose to allow the system to re-balance itself. However, I had been on an anti-depressant which did not take kindly to being stopped suddenly. It was a medication which you had to withdraw from over time. I suffered terribly from the medication withdrawal; I was all over the place; I was very poorly. The problem was that the staff did not know me well enough to know that it was not in my nature to be verbally aggressive, agitated and breaking things. All of which I am still somewhat ashamed to say I did because it is just so not how I behave, but I was really ill. Friends that visited me knew I was not at all myself but the hospital did not seem to accept there was this additional problem. I remember one day looking in the mirror in my room, and although the mirror was perfect I felt like the image I was seeing was really cracked and broken. At night I would spend hours sitting at the table in the dining room writing lists…lists of who would have what, because I was convinced I couldn't make it. It isn't like I had anything of great value even! But my mind was fixed on needing to sort out what would happen to my things and what I wanted to happen when I died. I collected angels for a long time and I remember I wrote everyone who attended my funeral was to be given one of my angels to remember me by. I was leaving my jewellery to Sophie, not that it was anything grand! Or I would be colouring in pictures, which felt safe. My mother brought me a colouring book and some felt-tip pens…on the inside cover she had written 'Create loads of pictures in your own colours. Create a world full of brightness within this book. Remember not all things are black and not all things are white. You are the colours of my life'. Reflecting on my time in hospital now as I write this book, I am still saddened by how unwell I was and I'm still angered by the treatment or lack of treatment I received during one of the worst times of my life. One evening I telephoned the minister from church, I was so distressed, and I was asking if he would come to see me. It was late at night and, of course, he couldn't come! However, he later told me he had telephoned the office to speak to the nurses. He said they assured him I was in my room and I was absolutely fine…he knew I wasn't; he knew I was in the dining room and very distressed because we had just spoke on the phone! I had a very turbulent time in the ward: some of the nurses were wonderful and some were just indifferent. Evening times would be covered mostly by agency staff who didn't know who was who! I continued to self-harm on the ward, sometimes breaking a cup to use. One time I got told by a nurse if I wanted to harm myself that was OK, but not if I was breaking hospital property. What a message…the cup has more value to us than your wellbeing! One of the most painful aspects of recovering from attempted suicide is having to see all the people that you would have left behind. See the pain and upset etched on their faces. Some of my friends would arrive to see me and burst into tears. That was very difficult, to see what my actions had done to them. Even though at the time I was extremely unwell, that doesn't make it any easier to see their pain. Thank heavens for Chris downstairs in the Psychology department, who did know me really well. Sophie, Jane and other friends were wonderful in visiting me and loving me through it. I was discharged after a few weeks; again it felt too soon and not on good terms! I later went through the complaints procedure and took it to the Mental Health Act Commission about the way in which I was treated by some members of the staff. I then took it as far as the Health Care Commission. My experience of the acute care ward really was not good at all. That is my biggest fear even now – that I don't get a really bad depression again and have to end up in the unit. Thankfully now I get down days or maybe a down week but it usually picks up again. I do start to panic if it stays any longer. Depression is like an uninvited guest that arrives without warning and leaves without notice. I am so pleased to be able to say that my life has moved on immensely. I am sure there are many people who have a much more positive experience of inpatient mental health care than my own. But I do know there are many people who come up against the same kinds of issues as I did. The hospital should be a place of refuge, a place to mend, a safe place; for me as an inpatient I don't feel it was any of those things. On the lowest day of my entire life I was sat before a duty psychiatrist who gave me the decision of whether or not I would be admitted to hospital. I needed that decision taken from me and made for me at that point – I was at the complete end of myself. Instead of that he told me if I wanted his help to stop seeking his attention with my questions. I am still angry about the way in which I was treated at that time and also during my time on the wards. We have come a long way in the treatment of mental health but I still feel that for some of us we have a way to go. In my experience most of the nursing staff spent their time in the office: what about interacting with the patients? Nights were often staffed by agency nurses who were often half asleep themselves. They had to come and ask our names as they did not know who was who. Is this really the correct level and quality of care for patients who are acutely unwell? I am sorry that I cannot write more positively about my experiences of inpatient care but these are my experiences. Thank goodness for a few really dedicated nursing staff that made a difference when they were on shift, for they seemed genuinely interested in the patients. One nurse in particular, Eddie, was such a genuine and lovely person; he always came and greeted you, always gave you a smile. I remember one morning I was walking down the corridor and I said good morning to one of the patients as I did every morning. This particular morning the man replied to me with a similar greeting. The nurse who heard him was so surprised because the patient was known to very rarely speak. I had not done anything special by any means. All I had done was greet him each morning and night; it didn't matter to me that I never got a reply. Then that one day he rewarded me with a response. Another time a dispute with some of the patients ended peacefully when the 'singing patient' was moved to the room next to mine. This patient would sing during the night, often the same few lines over and over again. It had bothered many of the patients and made them angry. For me it was something of a blessing; I found it would soothe me to sleep! Something which still reminds me of being in the hospital is white plastic cutlery: I really to this day don't like it; touching it really makes me remember and feel what it was like to be there. One evening Jane had been visiting me and was one of the last visitors to leave the ward that evening. As Jane waited by the doors to be let out, a nurse approached her and told her she couldn't leave; she needed to return to her room. That has been a source of much amusement between us! On another occasion I caused some panic unknowingly to me when I was left out to go for a brief walk. I had wandered over to the hospital chapel because it was peaceful...so peaceful in fact that I fell fast asleep! I should feel like the inpatient ward is somewhere that if I was ever extremely unwell again I would be cared for, but I don't feel like that. I think it is a dreadful situation when you end up having to question and challenge the very people who are in place to care for you because they failed in that duty of care. My mother overcame some of her own childhood bad memories to come and visit me in the mental health unit. The first time she visited she was breathing quite fast with anxiety; it must have been very difficult to come back to after being taken to visit her mum as a little girl. At least she could see a very different set up from the days of patients in rows in the corridor. I was very fortunate with visitors; one day I had some in each visiting room because I had too many at once. Here are a few poems that I have not previously shared which reflect on my time in hospital.

New admission to the ward...
Which label or category?
Which 'box' can we fit this one in?
Manic depression, schizophrenia, BPD?
The bad, the desperate, the sad.
Once you have a label we know which pills you need.
If you are feeling ill in between times...
If you are struggling...
Just don't bother us and please keep it neat
And tidy if you should bleed.

~

Across the car park broken legs, fractured bones, sores.
And wounds all treated accordingly.
Now for fractured minds, broken dreams, sore relationships,
The emotional casualty.
Tell me why one department is socially acceptable.
Whilst the other is 'taboo'.
Don't squeeze us into a box.
Don't make me a label.
Do not dispose of us in your mind.
You have no idea what people have been through.
Physical casualty – emotional casualty.
One and the same.
Fixing people in distress, tending to the sickness.
And releasing them from pain.

~

I was discharged from the hospital that second time like someone putting out the rubbish…that is how it felt to me at the time. I left hospital with broken toes where I had kicked the door in such anger and frustration. Plus I was still feeling quite physically unwell. I was also officially homeless again. I had to go straight from the hospital on the bus to the local housing office and once again declare myself homeless. I found it hard to face alone. I was given another room in another bed and breakfast. I went to the new house; I went into the room but I didn't want to be there: I didn't feel I could stay in yet another strange place. I couldn't face being alone again with my thoughts. Again the despair was creeping in and I didn't know what to do with myself. I walked around for a while, got a bus back to where I was most familiar with. But I didn't know what to do when I got there. I ended up calling '999' to tell them I would be found dead sometime that day because I couldn't make it. This was the person the hospital had discharged that morning as a well person. The police came and found me: they were very nice and they took me to my doctor's surgery. The doctor I saw said he couldn't do anything for me and that he too was having a bad day! I also saw the minister from church, who tried to help me also to see a future and possibilities. All I could see was my only option of being dead. From there I left and took myself home to my parents' house. It must have been dreadful for friends to worry about if I would be okay or not. I stayed at my parents' house for a few months, sleeping on a little two seater sofa. I spent my days colouring in pictures as I had done in the hospital. I liked colouring: it was safe and soothing. My mum looked after me in those first few months. Everyday things that we do all the time felt like such an effort. Things like going around the supermarket, and if it was busy I just couldn't stand it at all. It would take me several minutes to choose something which you would usually decide on in a split second or so. Just getting dressed and brushing my hair felt tiring. It seems so kind of crazy now as I write about it, because, like I said, we routinely just do these things. I felt like I had no purpose other than to get

from one end of the day to the other because I
knew people around me wanted me to. It wasn't
something I felt that I wanted for quite a long time
afterwards: I had lost any sense of purpose. I didn't
know if I would ever gain it back again or even that
I wanted to. It was hard work for the people around
me, I'm sure, but also for me too. My mother did a
complete U-turn about the anti-depressants, having
always been very against them. Instead, if I was
having a really bad morning she would ask if I had
taken my tablet…like it was some kind of miracle
cure…you popped it in and then you smiled. I
attended the day hospital, where I did pottery
classes and other activities. But just as on the ward
it was sometimes difficult to be around other people
who were very poorly. Most importantly of all, I
continued my work with Chris. Sophie and Jane
were really kind and helpful; they would come and
take me out. This had been without a doubt one of
the worst times in my life: I had been so unwell and
so not myself. My thinking was so scattered, and it
is kind of scary to look back at how ill I was. Also, I
no longer had my job with the school, a job that I
had loved. It was something, like I said, that I had
always wanted to do…now I had to find the wanting
within me to make it through the days. I really did
not know what I was going to do and in many ways
I felt my life was pretty much finished. Now I see
other people going through really testing
experiences and I wish that I could show them how
it was for me and how it changes with the passage
of time. It is so hard, sometimes impossible, to see
the changing landscape when we are caught in the
eye of the storm. Recently a dear friend of mine

said to me 'I wish I had your life', and I replied, 'I spent so long wishing I had somebody else's life'.

After a lot encouragement, and maybe a little persuasion, from Chris, I agreed to try some group therapy. I was part of a survivor's therapy group for three months. I was always extremely reluctant to take part in 'group' therapy, as I had never felt comfortable in groups of people before. To this day I am glad that I did take part in it: the main thing I took away from that experience was the knowledge that as a survivor I was not alone. I had read many books about other survivors but I had never knowingly met another survivor until then. It was a small group of six women and we bonded amazingly during our time in the sessions. It was such a relief to hear other women voicing some of the things I had kept in my own head for years. Hearing them vocalise some of my own thoughts and fears made me realise I was not the only one thinking and feeling as I did. It also meant a lot for me to meet another survivor whose abuser was a sibling. Up to that point, in the majority of the literature I had read the abuser was always described as the parent or grandparent...not often was being abused by a sibling mentioned. Since then I have gone on to learn that being abused by a sibling is a lot more common than you may first think. We built a lovely friendship and we remain in contact. There is quite a special almost unspoken bond between survivors. You know more than most how the other person has suffered and how they may be left feeling. For me, without a doubt, the hardest part of group therapy was hearing the other women tell their own stories. To hear firsthand what had happened to the others and to be in the room, to feel and see their pain and distress…that was really tough. They were courageous and strong women to be admired. On the last day of group therapy we had to pass around pieces of paper with each other's names on…and we had to write a comment for each person…we were then given these to take away with us…I still have mine now and I will always treasure it. I have always felt very fortunate with the opportunities to heal given to me as an adult by the NHS (other than as an inpatient!). I know for other survivors in different areas resources are not the same. Having been aware of that I always tried to make the most of the opportunities given to me. I would encourage survivors to try different forms of therapy but always ensure it was provided by valid and reputable sources. I myself have benefited from several different forms of therapy. Sometimes survivors tell me that they tried therapy 'once' and it was not for them. But sometimes it may just be that you can't get a rapport with a particular therapist or that the method of therapy may not be the right one for you at that time. As a survivor of childhood abuse you deserve the opportunity to make sense of and mend from the trauma; seek the help you need and deserve.

Once the group therapy was complete I resumed my sessions with Chris. One of my toughest, but one that brought me I think the most freedom inwardly, was working on my inner child. In the early days of working on my inner child it was with great reluctance and hesitation on my part. I hated my inner child and therefore I hated myself. The last thing I wanted to do was to have anything to do with her, let alone embrace her so that she could mend. It took months for me to change how I felt about 'little me'. I needed to be angry with her and I needed her to know that she was bad and deserved to be punished. I thought there must have been something about her that made Joe abuse her as he had. I was even angry with her for being in the house, for being alone upstairs so that it could happen. Until I came to realise that I was just being a child, I was living my life, I was upstairs sleeping or playing; I was doing what children do. I did not ask to be abused and I did not deserve to be. Mostly I used writing to communicate back and forth a dialogue between my adult self and 'little me'. It is interesting to look back at those poems now and see the very real changes that happened during the course of those writings. I couldn't even bring myself to look at her face; it was too painful, too difficult. Yet I came to realise that if I did not accept and begin to look after my inner child, nobody else was going to. I was all that she had and, likewise, she was all that I had. Inside of me was a very hurt little girl and I had to learn to accept her and want to allow her to heal so that I could heal too. I had to stop blaming her/myself for the things which had happened to me as a child. Also, the words of my mum in those earlier years about only liking good girls had trickled deep into the heart of me, and I had to work on realising that I had been a regular child. In one of my poems it begins...'Bad girl, what did you do to make your mother hate you…? The answer is I was not a bad girl and I did nothing to warrant any hate. Chris told me on many occasions that if I was able to meet my inner child's needs she would go quiet; she would melt into my adult self and let me be at peace. Whilst I was not convinced at the time…Chris was right. The way I understood it was that if we as children have really crucial, unmet emotional needs these can be carried over into our adult selves and that inner child remains inside of us until the needs are met. First I began not to hate mine and then I began to reason with her; finally I accepted her and agreed to help her find what she needed.

Hello, Little Girl…

Didn't anyone ever tell you what happened is not your fault?
Didn't anyone ever tell you those scars you carry can heal?
Didn't anyone ever tell you how precious you are?
Didn't anyone ever tell you how much you are loved and wanted?
Didn't anyone ever tell you you're not alone?
Didn't anyone ever tell you that you were born for so much more than this?
Then let me be the one to tell you.

~

It can be so hard having to be a 'grown up' when there is a frightened little girl inside of you who wants someone to hold her hand. Sometimes you don't want to be the adult because you feel like a very vulnerable child. Now I try to remember all the lovely things about my childhood and I have Sophie to help me remember the things I have long forgotten. It was not by any means all bad and it is good to think about the happy times. Something which I do from time to time is look up my favourite children's programmes on the internet! They make me feel all happy and safe just as they did when I was a child. Television was often a very happy escape from reality. The time when I feel I sort of revert back to feeling childlike is when I'm physically not well. I think it is that feeling of a lack of control with my body. That feeling that something is happening to me which I can do little about. Even now I want my mum when I'm sick! I want her to come and tuck me in and bring me Lucozade! We always got Lucozade when we were poorly. In the glass bottle with the yellow-coloured cellophane wrapped around it!

Another healing tool for me was 'Art Therapy'. People often think that they have to be able to draw and paint to do art therapy. But it's not about artistic ability: its being able to express what you are feeling through using different art mediums. Art therapy gives you the space to reflect and to bring out from inside of you whatever you choose on that given day. Some sessions were structured, but mostly we were given the freedom to choose what paper we wanted: size, colour, thin paper or card. The same with paints, pencils, crayons...I often went for the paints...two colours, black and red! Sometimes it was a little in-joke between the group and they would automatically hand me the black and red paints. One of my favourite paintings from this time is one which is like a woven mat and it has all different colours going through it. This was to remind me and others that life isn't just black and white (as it often is when we become very depressed in our thinking). Life has many beautiful colours and I always want to remember that. Sometimes I shocked myself with what actually did emerge onto my piece of paper. For example, the painting of me under the table and all the shouting around me that I talked about earlier in this book. I am glad that I did art therapy and I am also very glad that I didn't dispose of my work, which I almost did once or twice over the last few years. I also used some of the pottery sessions during my time at the day hospital like an art therapy. On days when I was feeling extremely low I always seemed to revert back to making little figures, often without faces. When I look at them now some of them do seem quite disturbing! At the time when I made them they just felt kind of familiar to me. Looking at them now I realise how much I was hurting inside.

A lump of clay…
Shapeless and cold.
But ready to be used.
Full of potential
To become something useful.
Something beautiful.
Life…
Like that shapeless lump of clay,
Waiting for energy,
Waiting for inspiration,

Kate Swift

Can become useful.
Can become beautiful.
Some will look and just see a mass of 'clay'.
Some will look and just see 'mental illness'.
But YOU are a masterpiece in the making.

~

So life was moving along: I was getting support from the day hospital as a day patient; I had my sessions with Chris and I was trying to find my feet again. A few months after leaving the hospital I was fortunate to be offered a home of my own. It was a one bedroom flat on what locally was a very undesirable estate to live on. I went to view the flat and of course Sophie came too: she was my support and my security blanket! The flat was in a very poor and neglected state: the walls were not just grubby; they were filthy, dirty, as were the ceilings to match! But it would be mine…my own space…my own little place to call home.

I was very hesitant about accepting it because it was so grim-looking, but Sophie in her wisdom encouraged me to go for it. So three months after leaving hospital I had a flat to rent. Sophie and I set to work cleaning and painting. My dad and Sophie's dad both lent a hand with some of the decorating. Slowly but surely it came together as each room became clean, freshly painted, and began to look like a home. It was a lot of work and it took a lot of elbow grease to make it fit to live in but together we did it. The first night I slept in the flat I remember I woke up about 3 am and I went into the sitting room, switched the light on and stood looking at the room thinking…it's mine…my home. It was lovely to have a place to call my home. Friends were understandably a bit nervous about me living alone again but I was happy to feel like I finally have a space of my own. I loved the sense of security and yet freedom. I could make the rules and one of them was that people were not going to shout and argue in my home. At first you have to get used to different noises, and I faced them head on: if something was bothering me I went to investigate what it was…because I was determined that I was going to feel totally safe in my own home. One of the things I love the most about my home…Joe has never been in it. The flat gave me a security that I had not felt in a very long time and was a wonderfully healing thing in itself. It wasn't all plain sailing but at last I felt I had a base to begin again. It was so nice to have all of my things around me after over six months of sleeping in the temporary accommodation, the hospital, or on the two-seater sofa at my parents' house. One thing which I haven't yet been able to change is sleeping with my bedroom door open, even though it is my home: I have to have my bedroom door shut tight at night. Somewhere deep inside of me is that little girl who thinks if the door is left open you won't hear anyone coming into the room. Having the door shut tight feels like I am shutting all the bad things outside. I moved into the flat with my wardrobe, chest of drawers, a portable television and personal belongings. No bed, no cooker etc, and just gradually bit by bit I put a home together, with the help of friends. I was so fussy about the flat being perfectly tidy…not a thing out of place…again trying to feel that sense of control. I am much more relaxed about it these days but I was a bit obsessive about my cleaning: my flat was constantly 'bleached'! One of my good friends even wrote a poem about my love affair with the bleach bottle! Which I thought was great fun!

Kate Swift

Eau de Toilet

My friend wears her obsession.
No, not the one by Calvin Klein.
Hers comes from the Spaniard, Dom Estos,
And smells "Original"? Or "Pine".
Every time she walks into a room
Ninety-nine percent of bacteria leave.
While one percent just get the hump.
When she rolls back her sleeves.

From banks of cushions on her sofa
She stares way out to see.
The tiniest speck of crumb or dust
An atoll missed by you or me.
She fights them with her bleaches.
And just when I think she's done,
Her dust-busting mini vac roars at her hip.
Her battle is never won.

She splashes it all over.
She'd sterilise the world,
If it would only stand still long enough.
Her duster waits unfurled.
To the dirt and grime of living.
Strong messages she sends.
She now has something "six times strength".
To help her round the bend.

My friend wears her obsession.
No, not the one by Calvin Klein.
Her eau de toilet is reminiscent of
Hospital corridors, past times.
Some might think she's rather strange.

I just think she's free.
And I feel very privileged.
That my obsessed friend loves me.

© Brian Barefield 2006

The flat went a long way to making me feel there was something to build upon again, but I was still in the grip of depression and it took a long time to climb out of that pit. I used an online support forum, which was such an amazing find at the time when I needed it the most. The people there were talking my language; they understood my feelings of despair. I made some lovely friends on the support forum and I spent many nights chatting until morning. I still maintain some of the friendships I made on that first forum. I will always remember it because it made such a difference to those long lonely nights when sleep eluded me. One of my friends shared a letter they wrote to 'The Beast'…the beast being the depression, and it made such perfect sense to me. It also made me want to win over my own battles with the beast. It was written by my good friend 'Solo', and with his permission I share it here with you in the hope it will help others as it did on the forum.

Open letter to: The Beast

I now see you for what you are. I won't hide from
you any longer or deny your existence.
You have destroyed my life by taking from me
everything that was dear to me. That was your
mistake.
Now I have nothing to lose and nothing to fear. I will
stare you right in the eye until you back down.
Little by little I will weaken you. Even though you
hide all positive things from my sight I will still know
they are there. I have seen them and made note of
them. Every time you make me feel bad I will find a
way to feel better. When you try to make me
destroy myself by telling me I am worthless I will
know it's you and reject the feeling. Without my co-
operation you are powerless. That's your true
weakness.

I will destroy all your power and keep you locked in
a dark corner of my mind as a trophy of my triumph.
I will then expose your weakness to others so they
can destroy your brethren.

In case you rear your ugly head again I will mount a
copy of this letter on my wall as a reminder of my
resolve to defeat you.
Your *former* slave
Solo

~

I also joined a support group for women who were
or had been in domestic abuse. Again it was hard

to listen to the other members telling their own stories. But it was insightful too and I was able to give some practical advice as well as gain something from it myself. As I got stronger I took myself out of the day hospital environment: I felt I needed to stand on my own. I continued my sessions with Chris up until his post came to an end at the hospital. It was immensely distressing to part from my therapy, but more so to part from someone who had changed my world so much from the inside out. We had done so much work, covered so much ground, and now I really was about to sink or swim. It was really tough at first; I missed the support, and I missed having that space to be heard. But we can't stay in therapy forever; we need to use the tools that we have learnt to make our own way in life and indeed to build our life. A life that is hopefully more stable and happy than the one which brought us to be in therapy in the first place. From that time to this present day I have been busy 'swimming'. I felt I owed it to all the people who had put so much energy into helping me to press on and make something positive out of all the negative.

In recent years my father's health has declined a great deal. My mother still is at home looking after him, more than ever now. As an adult I have had a very neutral relationship with my dad. Once I left home it was much easier to only be visiting rather than living with his mood swings which continued all through my years of growing up. Sophie can also testify to my father's moods! She has seen them on many occasions. Yet she also agrees with me about his humour and wit, that when he is on form it is razor sharp and very funny. When I visited we made very general conversation either about the weather, local events or the grandchildren. The odd thing to me is that whilst I never felt I had a daddy, my dad has been a loving grandfather who has spent time with the grandchildren. He walked around the garden with his granddaughter collecting ladybirds! I have always felt glad for the grandchildren that they have a nice bond with their granddad. All of the grandchildren are very fond of him and I think that is ideally how it should be. I am not bitter towards my dad; I don't have strong negative feelings other than the sadness for what never was. I did very much so growing up always want a daddy and I didn't see a 'daddy' figure was ever going to be possible with my dad. Yet my sister is the opposite: she was, as I said earlier in the book, a daddy's girl and I was always mummy's girl, which caused untold sibling fractures between us. Just this past year has been a giant shift in my interaction with my dad due to his physical health. That man who was loud, angry, powerful, controlling, when I was a small girl, is now totally dependent on those around him for everything he needs. During his long stay in hospital I visited every other day, not because I felt I had to out of duty but because I wanted to. Now when I visit my dad seems genuinely pleased to see me and I get a sense of gentleness that I've never had before. Sometimes when I am ready to leave he will want me to stay longer, and secretly I relish that because for the first time in my life I feel wanted by him. Last Christmas that same sense of humour played out as I was visiting dad in hospital. He was in a wheelchair and I was showing him some Christmas decorations. Dad got the gold tinsel and wrapped it all around himself and we were all amused. To me there would be no point in being bitter; the only person I would be hurting is myself. I just try to embrace the situation as it stands now and be the daughter. Seeing my father as he is now is very difficult; it is so painful to watch someone so physically incapacitated. To think about all the simple things in life that my dad will never again be able to do. Recently I was standing at a local bus stop – it is beside a green – dad used to walk over the green to buy the newspaper…and one minute I was waiting for my bus; the next I had tears streaming down my face as I realised dad would never again be able to do that. Simple things do mean a lot and it is a reminder to me not to take the little things for granted. One morning my dad went out as usual, no signs that anything was wrong: he walked up just two roads from home and then collapsed in the street with a massive stroke. Life changed forever as quickly as the flick of a switch.

The question of 'forgiveness' is one that comes up time and again within the realms of healing from childhood abuse. Although, never in my therapy was I challenged to forgive. I have done some forgiving on the journey…to myself. I had to forgive the fifteen-year-old school girl who I felt could and should have done better in her school exams. I had to forgive the twenty-one year old for making bad relationship choices. I had to forgive myself along this path many times, but to forgive my abuser…for me the answer is no. Here was somebody who had taken away half of my childhood and left me with a living nightmare to try to wake up from. He has never once shown remorse, never said or acted sorry. Indeed he tried to abuse me again after my six months in foster care. Is that the actions of someone who acknowledges the wrong they did and wants to make any kind of peace? I think too much pressure can be put on survivors to forgive people. If Joe came to me tomorrow and apologised would it mean anything to me? The answer is no, it would not. Even when he left home, he brought his girlfriend round to the house and was intimate with her in the room just next to mine. He also delighted in telling crude jokes to my father in my presence. All of these behaviours do not strike me as someone who is sorry for their behaviour and aware of the damage it caused. If anything he was smug, arrogant and sometimes offensive. I know some survivors who have forgiven their abuser, and all power to them. In some ways I consider them to be a greater person than I am for being able to do that. I think the question of forgiveness is a very personal one for each individual. If it is something you feel called or need to do for your own sake then all power to you, providing it is for the right reasons. I cannot know if I will feel differently in the years to come. Joe went on to have two children with his partner and that is the only time I wanted something from Joe…I wanted him to be a good dad to those children, to give them a beautiful childhood, one I never had. That is all I want from him, nothing else. Of course Joe having children of his own opens up many more questions with regards to safety. I have done as much as I can to ensure the well being and welfare of his children. It has been an extremely difficult path to walk along; it is out of respect and love for his children that I have not written about them further in this book. I am told he is rehabilitated. Can I accept that deep down inside myself...I am not convinced; I wish that I was. Whilst I can think about the boy who suffered abuse at the hands of Mr X and feel sorrow for him, I cannot separate that from what he went on to do to me. Ask me anything about my experiences and I will tell you if I can...just do not ask me to forgive. Some people assume that because I say I don't wish to forgive that I am eaten up with anger and hatred, but I hope you can see through this book that I am not. I would not want to fill my head up with hating him: what would be the point? What good would it do me? Of course I have strong feelings about what happened, but I believe to be hateful on a regular basis would just turn me into a bitter person. Yet nothing can restore to me the years that I feel have been swallowed up trying to just get from one day to the next. I feel like I lost so much of my childhood, teens and twenties. I recently had a conversation with the minister from church who pointed out that I was actually living like someone who had forgiven, interesting thought. I guess not being hateful and seeking revenge is a form of forgiveness, but I live this way for my sake and most certainly not for his.

~

Kate Swift

What you did will never be alright.
The innocence you stole in the still of the night.
Every year that passes by does not diminish what
you did to me.
I am no longer in chains but I am still not fully free.
Time is not going to wipe away your debt.
Time is not going to allow me to forget.
I am never going to be able to reconcile a little girl's
mind.
After everything you did so painful and unkind.
If I lived a thousand years it would still never be
alright.
The innocence you stole in the still of the night..

~

My peaceful beach, my solitude.
Then sweeps in the memories.
Painful, sharp, cold and crude.
Creeping in like the tide.
Flooding my mind.
Making me feel sick inside.
Suddenly my beach is a sea of carnage.
Angry waves are lapping at my feet.
I want to turn and flee to a place of retreat.
Save me before I drown in the sea of yesterday.
Save my little girl before he steals her away..

~

UNFORGIVEN
Do I forgive you?
For pinning me down.
Taking my innocence.

Nobody's Rag Doll

Raping my childhood.
Stealing my teens.
Sending me to a living hell.
Tormented out of my soul.
No.
You will forever be
UNFORGIVEN.

~

I could not write such a book without including one
of my dearest friends. Her middle name was
'Primrose' because she was born on Primrose Day.
I came to be knocking on her door to deliver some
church flowers to her as she lived very near my
parents when I lived at home. I got the warmest
welcome, a lovely cup of tea and a friendly chat.
That was to be the first of hundreds of visits to see
Molly. Molly knew of my family name: most people
did where I grew up because of Charlie! Molly told
me she had always thought that Charlie was an
only child because she only ever saw him out on
the streets. That is because as desperately as my
mother tried there was no keeping him in. Molly told
me about seeing Charlie sitting on the pavement as
a boy, digging up the freshly laid tarmac with a
stick! She told him he best put it all back again and
make it right otherwise his mother would get a bill
from the Council to mend the pavement…and he
fixed it. It was fascinating to hear about my own
family from someone outside of the circle. Although
Molly was in her 80's we built the most amazing
bond between us. I knew that there would always
be a smile, a caring face and a hug waiting for me

at Molly's house. I felt so warm, wanted and secure when I was at Molly's. I would say to my mum 'I'm just popping round the corner to see Molly; I won't be long" and then I would return three–four–five hours later. I helped sometimes with practical things around the house and Molly helped me to see the world as a nicer place. I had never before had someone invest so much time and love in me as Molly did. We would talk for hours and I loved looking at old photographs, hearing all the stories behind them of times gone by. As I write about my dear friend my eyes are brimming with tears as Molly is no longer with us. Molly was one of life's true diamonds: although she never ever thought of herself as special, she was special. She was a real people person, always thinking of others and always ever ready to help anyone if she could. Molly put a lot of love and care into my life; she was I know extremely fond of me and I of her. Some of my best times were the times Molly would tell me stories about the war years. It was fascinating as she recounted living through the blitz in the very area I grew up in. Not just living through it but being an active part of fire watching duty amongst other duties. Of getting an old pram and knocking door to door to fill the pram up with baby things for a mother and baby who had been bombed out of their home. I spent many happy hours in a cosy chair with a cup of tea listening to Molly and her history. At Christmas time Molly had a present for everyone – and I do mean everyone…the delivery boy, the milkman, the staff at the chemist, and so on. I would begin wrapping presents for Molly in early October and get finished in December when her spare bedroom would be full to bursting with presents. Molly didn't forget people and she valued everyone the same no matter what. I remember fondly my times in church sitting next to her, and she would say to me "And I want to hear you sing"! Because I used to mime as my singing is dreadful! Molly's sitting room was full wall to wall of family photographs; she adored her family with a passion. Molly taught me about politics and many other worldwide important issues. She had a wonderful way of explaining the most complicated issues so that they made perfect sense to me. Molly taught me practical things too like pastry making! I remember her being horrified when I said 'You go and buy an apple pie from the freezer department of the supermarket'. Although ill-health restricted her she never let it get her down; she was always smiling, joking and singing. Molly had such a giggle at me and her home help trying on her different hats from over the years. We had many laughs together and some tears too. I miss her hand, all aged with the passage of time and yet able to slip into mine and grip it in a way that said 'I know and I love you'. I miss the hugs; Molly gave great hugs. She was a really beautiful soul, one of the very best. She will always be extremely dear to my heart and I am so glad to be able to tell you about her. If I am half the person she was when I am in my later years, well, then I will be doing alright. The last time I saw Molly was in the hospital. I was leaving her room and I turned and looked back…I blew molly a kiss and she blew me one back. A short time after this I read a saying, 'Don't cry because it's over, smile because it happened', and that is so very true. I know that if Molly was here today she would be so proud of the things I have been doing this year. When I gave my first radio interview I got a photo of us down from the shelf and placed it right in front of me on the desk. I was so nervous but Molly and I got through it together. All through my life I will carry Molly with me right inside my heart; the world was a far richer place when Molly was here. I am thankful to still be in touch with Molly's daughters and one of her granddaughters, which means a lot to me. When I wrote about Molly for the church magazine I said she would always continue to positively influence my life, and five years on that is exactly so.

I look heavenwards.

Wanting.

Longing.

Hoping.

Dreaming.

Wishing.

Willing.

To have you here with me.

~

Between Friends

Such wonderful conversation we have shared.
We have talked and talked…we have truly cared.
We have remembered the years now rolling by.
We have sat and held hands, allowed the other to
cry.
We have laughed and laughed until the tears of joy
rolled,
& talked with energy uncontrolled.
We have shared a worry, a problem and a
heartache.
We have been real, so real it could never be fake.
We have talked over photographs and yesterday's
news.
We have debated politics and other views.
We have talked in silence; in silence there is a word
Held between two friends and always heard.
We have talked with you in a hospital bed
somewhat weary,
& me at your bedside, words failing me and all
teary.
It is our last conversation I hold so very dear in my
heart.
The words of symbols…a kiss blown to you…blown
back to me.
Our final conversation before us two friends did
part.
Alas, we still talk now in my mind…
& there you are still you and I have not left you
behind.

~

Kate Swift

Memories

Memories are the pictures stored and buried in your
mind.
Some are warm.
Some are precious.
Some are painful and unkind.
They are the remainders of yesterday.
They are the reminders that nothing gold can stay.
A sensation of warmth or a twinge of pain.
A place to hold people dear.
A place sometimes shadowed with doubt and fear.
To dwell on special moments; your mind is a
wonderful room.
Where you can find the people and times that were
gone too soon.

~

Give me one more day.
One more squeeze of the hand.
One more cuddle.
One more smile.
One more laugh.
One more song.
One more cup of tea.

Give me one more day.
To be with her.
To talk with her.
To listen to her.
To see her smile.
To see her face.
To feel that warmth.

Just one more day.

~

A few years back I was engaged to a nice guy. He was not abusive in any way and I knew then that I had broken the chain of abusive relationships. We had a good relationship on the whole, and I thought that I had finally found the person I was going to settle with. He was totally besotted with me and would have done anything for me (within reason!). The problem was that whilst I loved him, I realised I was not 'in' love with him. Sophie could see it too; she used to tell me that she could see I didn't feel about him how I should. But because previous relationships had been so bad and this was so different in comparison, I thought this was it. I thought this was as good as it gets in a healthy relationship. Over time I realised it wasn't working for me and that perhaps it could be even better than this. I want to fall in love and be loved in equal measure. I now think enough of myself to not settle for something that isn't healthy or isn't right for me, and that is a really big change in my thinking. From the eighteen-year-old who begged her abusive and violent partner not to leave her because she felt she 'needed him'. I am very happy and secure in my own company, which means I will never 'need' a relationship in that way again. This I believe frees you up to be in a relationship because you choose to be and because it is right for you.

Love is happy, joyful and bright.

In caring and giving it takes its delight.
Love sees no race, colour or creed.
It only sees what the heart needs.
Love does not intentionally cause pain.
It seeks out the sunshine, does not dwell on the rain.
True love does not cause a bruise or a heart to ache.
It binds together; it does not break
Love is not selfish; love is not about 'I' or 'ME'.
Love does not stand for captivity.
Love is happy, joyful and bright.
In caring and giving it takes its delight.

~

Creativity makes me feel really alive; it is hard to put into words. Some of my happiest moments are alone with nature and my camera. In the midst of depression we can be robbed of our ability to see life in all its vibrant colours; like our thinking at that time, life can feel varying shades of grey. Through my photography I seek to capture moments full of brightness, beauty, life in all its glory. We all at times need reminding that the world around us is still a beautiful place.

Step off the carousel of life.

Step outside the daily toil and strife.

Take time to feel the sun on your face.

To walk in a beautiful place.

Nobody's Rag Doll

To watch the world go by.

To see the birds soaring in the sky.

It is a peace that every soul yearns for day by day.

Time to be still, to watch and to play.

~

Today I flee into the open arms of nature,
& I am embraced fully...
Held in awesome wonder at this world's beauty.
I come with all my winter pain and sorrowing.
I am taken and led on tiptoe gently into spring.
Free to taste the mystery of bud, blossom and
seed.

Drinking in peace for a soul in need.
Bathing in the rainbow colours, splashed all around.
Feeling the earth beneath my feet...
Reassuring solid ground.
Watching the birds soar, and as they rise
My heart slowly steadily rises too...
Immersed in nature
I am nurtured.
I am whole again.
I am made new.

~

It was at the start of '2010' that I finally felt able to
fulfil my desire in sharing my poetry with other
survivors. That is how 'This Tangled Web' came
into being as I created my website, a platform to
share and to reach other survivors of childhood
sexual abuse. In the first six months of opening the
online support group and social networking account
for 'This Tangled Web', over 500 people have
crossed my path. If I had only reached one survivor
it would all have been worthwhile. Also during

2010, I had my poetry accepted by 'Chipmunka' publishers to have my own book. That again felt very validating of my feelings and my experiences. That in itself is healing, to have totally independent people choose to stand with you in something so deeply personal. It was a very exciting moment to hold my book in my hands for the first time…I remember thinking 'Wow, it's a 'real' book with a cover and pages!' I felt a sense of achievement, but also overwhelming sadness that I had not been able to write a book about 'happy' things, and also that my family remain living in denial and would not be sharing in the achievement. One day I aim to write that 'happy' book, although this one is very much about surviving and overcoming personal challenges…and that has to be a good thing!

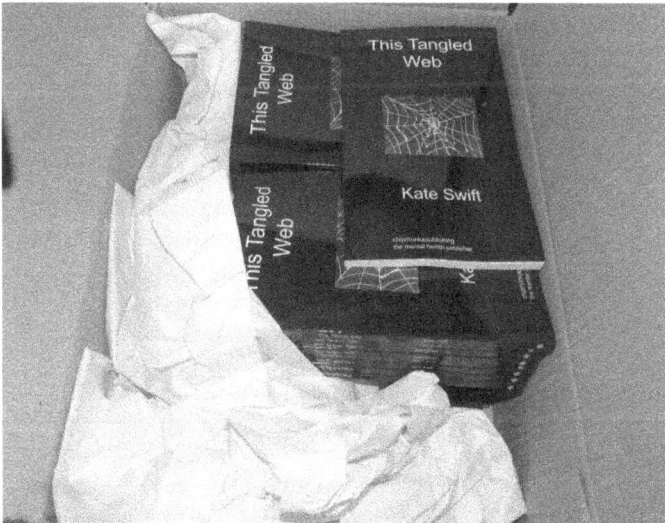

(My First Delivery of Books)

The book launch was a great opportunity to mark how far I have come, not just this year but on this long and challenging journey. It was such a pleasure to be able to personally hand a copy of my first book to my former psychologist. It was such a joy to see Chris again and in such different circumstances. It felt liberating to be so public about my past and, yes, a little scary too! Many friends, former colleagues and others were unaware of my background until I chose to tell them since building 'This Tangled Web'. Also, I have had some really moving emails and messages from people who have come across the website. It is my pleasure to share a handful of the comments with you...

'I sat in total amazement as if it was written for me, but only it was a neighbour and not my brother. You speak the words of a lot of victims and if I had difficulty voicing them I could just point to your poetry.'

'I read Family Denial and Rejection – it made me cry with how it resonated with my truth. Truth was always elusive in my family...Thank you for my voice.'

'Sometimes I find it hard to unblock the emotions and when I read your poems it helps as I really relate to you.'

'I cry when I read your work and your words. Not just tears of sadness or hurt, but also joy and gladness and relief that one day I will be further than I am now, as you are.'

'My copy of your book finally arrived. My husband has been reading it whilst I've been at work today. He said he felt angry and was tearful at times. It's giving him a much better insight and understanding of my feelings.'

When I started to write my story down I was really uncertain that I would be able to write it all the way through…and that I would have enough to share with you within the pages of a book. As I come to the end of telling you my story I have spent the last week feeling like a little girl again but she is now standing back and observing the wreckage that was her early years. I have had much sadness in my heart this week as I take in the scene of destruction. However, I think it is 'normal' and healthy to feel the sadness for a time; there is much loss to grieve for on revisiting. However, we (me and my inner child) survived it and have moved away from the centre of that chaos. My inner child can slip her hand into mine and together we continue walking to freedom. It has been challenging to share with you and yet a great opportunity to re-evaluate many events that have happened. To see things with the eyes and mind of an adult…to choose to look the past in the face and know it has lost its once vice-like grip on me and my future.

(Book Launch Photo)

I have become a very determined (and friends would say stubborn) person: if someone tells me I won't be able to do something, I become more determined that I can. Never in my wildest dreams would I at one time have believed that one day I would indeed be reaching survivors as I do today through my website, book and online group. I feel very privileged when a Survivor contacts me, and I have met the most amazing, courageous and warm people. It has been heart-warming to see all the work other individuals and groups are doing to make a real difference to the lives of children growing up now and also to adult survivors. We have come a long way and yet we have a long way to go. There is much work to be done and there is a peaceful army of willing people wanting to make a difference.

Just as in my last book 'This Tangled Web', I make the point that I am not completely healed…but I am no longer totally broken. I think healing is a continuing journey when you have been deeply hurt. I used to be really bothered by the thought that however long I live, I will always have been an abused person; I can never take that away. But now I think however long I live I will be a survivor with abuse in her past and not her present. I have come such a long way in my healing. It can be really encouraging to look back and see how far you have come. Sometimes survivors tell me they cannot see progress for themselves, but they may have been really busy 'just' surviving and I know the energy that can take, and it isn't something to be under estimated. Can we ever be fully restored from the nightmare that is childhood abuse? Some survivors would say yes and part of me would love to agree, but for me I am not yet convinced. One thing I will always give you in this is my honesty, which is why the final chapter has both light and shade.

I believe life can be a hundred times better than you think it can be. I believe we can mend a great deal but our history will always be the same; we cannot rewrite it. We can through help change the way our history is stored in our mind. I like to think of it in picture language…imagine a filing cabinet that is overflowing with papers, so full that it cannot be properly closed and so the contents are always in our face to one degree or another…it feels cluttered and uncomfortable. That is how I feel my mind was! With help I took everything out of that filing cabinet: some of the contents I was able to throw away; some took a long time to work through…eventually my filing was much more organised and I was able to close it away. Close it so that it did not spill into my everyday existence as it once did. We can…and I urge all survivors to do this…change our future, and I know we can because I did. I can remember when I thought about what happened to me every single day and I thought I would never be free of it. Now I am choosing to think about it through my website, talking to survivors and my writing…it no longer invades my thinking as it once did. That is a big difference from where I felt it haunted me every day by invading my thoughts, and that was so draining at the time.

I do have the sensory reminders, which are still unpleasant but very manageable now. Such as the smell of coconut…he wore a coconut scented sun tan lotion in the summers. Or a certain type of bed cover: very random things to anyone reading this, but Survivors will know exactly what I mean. The other thing I have struggled with a great deal…and actually it is only in this last year I am starting to overcome it…saying my abuser's actual name out loud. For years I have referred to Joe as 'Him' or 'My Abuser' or 'my brother that abused me'. I don't like hearing his name but I am finding it easier to say it. For years I also struggled with the very words 'sexual abuse'. I have bucket loads more confidence than I ever had before. I used to believe that my life was finished, that nothing good could possibly come of it. Now I believe I can achieve and

I can make a difference, however small it may be. I used to walk down the street staring at the pavement, but now I am so much more aware of the world around me and my place in it.

I have been and am so very blessed with the most wonderful friends. Sophie, as I have talked about, is my dearest and oldest friend; I can't imagine life without her. Jane was a big part of my recovery in therapy and just a total rock so many times over. My friends have validated me as a person; they have validated what I have gone through and they have loved me for who I am. When I was a child I grew up fearing the world outside. I remember I used to think to myself – 'If that is what my family can do to me, what is the rest of the world going to do to me?' – but, you know something, I learnt that the rest of the world was not such a scary place after all; in fact it can be a darn sight nicer than the place you emerge from as a child.

I am free from many of the feelings I carried around inside of me for so long, having worked through them in therapy. I would love to be able to tell you that I am totally healed from what happened to me as a child, but that would not be the truth and I can only deal in truths. I am no longer plagued by nightmares, just one every now and again; I will wake up with my nail prints in the palm of my hand where I have been clenching my fist so tightly in my sleep. Occasionally I do get sad and I do think about the 'what ifs', but it is more fleeting now than it ever was before. When I am thrown back to a bad memory, I now see it as an opportunity to heal from it a little more each time it is revisited. I do believe the mind allows us to remember certain things as and when we are ready to process them or at least begin to.

As for Joe I do feel cheated; I feel like I never had my justice in a legal sense but at least I made myself heard at long last. I feel like through my recovery and my books I have gained a personal justice. Also, he will have to live with what he did for the rest of his life. I believe many survivors need to claim their personal justice as too often it is the only kind that we are going to have. Take every opportunity to heal and repair the damage that has been done to you...so you can stand strong and say of your abuser, 'You did not break me'...to me that is a personal justice worth claiming.

Life is so much better on many different levels and in different ways, big and small. For a long time my healing was greatly hampered by negativity around me...when I still lived at the often chaotic family home...when I was in abusive adult relationships...when people would undo the good work that had been done...we need to be aware of things which prevent us from healing. Nothing should stop us from healing our past if that is what we choose to do. We need supportive, loving, caring people around us...people who have our welfare and our best interests at heart. That gives a solid basis on which to mend and rebuild, but sometimes that loving, caring person may just be you alone...making the decision to give yourself a break and resolving to get the help you need. As a good friend of mine recently said: 'I've come to realise and learn that life is a gift. It is not the sort of gift that comes in a pretty box, decorated with a large bow and handed to you. It comes from hard work and honesty but the rewards are fantastic'. © Alison Harmer

The life I have now proves to me that you can overcome and have a richer life than you may have once thought was ever possible. As an adult you no longer have to be constrained by the things of your past; your life does not have to conform to those old rules and patterns. I feel like my own person at long last and I am most certainly nobody's rag doll anymore. I feel like I began my healing journey in the coldest, darkest wilderness in my soul and now the landscape has changed so much and I am able to feel the warmth of the sun. I have every reason to feel optimistic about the future. One of my own favourite sayings to myself is 'Tomorrow is a brand new day'…It is time to go out and chase those rainbows. I hope you will do the same: it is nothing less than you deserve.

Kate Swift

~

A Survivor Heart

I have the heart of a survivor.
It is brave, enduring and strong.

I have the heart of a survivor.
It is loving and giving despite your wrong.

I have the heart of a survivor.
Watch me achieve my dreams.

I stand strong in the broken places.
My heart is woven with courage at the seams.

~

Nobody's Rag Doll

It is time to throw away the old rule book, to kiss the
pain goodbye.

I am done with the history, no time now to sit and
cry.

With my head held high, I will stand on new and
solid ground.

I am away to chase the rainbows; I know they are
waiting to be found

I have an empty book to fill with memories shiny
and new.

Take my hand and come chase a rainbow too.

~

Contacting the Author…

My Website: www.thistangledweb.co.uk

You can contact the author of this book via email:
tangledweb010@yahoo.co.uk

You can also keep up to date on Twitter
'thistangledweb'

My first book…

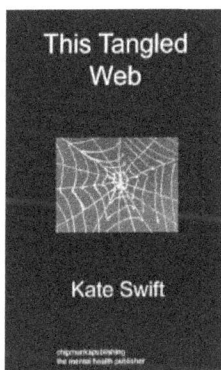

This Tangled
Web

Kate Swift

chipmunkapublishing
the mental health publisher

Available from Chipmunka, Amazon, Waterstones
and Tesco Online

Signed Copies are also available directly from our
online shop
www.thistangledweb.co.uk

All sales from the online shop are used to produce
more flyers, more posters, more events etc, to

promote awareness of Child Sexual Abuse and recovery.

Further sources of help and information:

Please note that whilst I have personally visited the sites listed below and recommend them, I would encourage you to use your own judgement when visiting as the contents may change over time, of which I have no control over. Please practice self-care when looking at material online.

Based in the United Kingdom:

www.napac.org.uk The National Association for People Abused in Childhood. Our Survivor Support Line telephone number is 0800 085 3330.

www.oneinfour.org.uk We provide a unique service to individuals, both directly and indirectly. Directly through individual therapy and helpline support. Indirectly through campaigning, policy making, in-house research, training, and consultancy work with statutory and non-statutory agencies.

www.oneinfour.org Ireland

www.nshn.co.uk The National Self Harm Network…Supports, Empowers and Educates.

www.loveshouldnthurtyou.co.uk A website dedicated to helping and raising awareness about domestic violence with a specific focus on educating teenagers.

www.nexusinstitute.org The NEXUS Institute works across Northern Ireland to respond to the needs of adults who have experienced sexual abuse, violence or rape.

Nexus Institute
119 University Street
Belfast
BT9 1HP
Tel: 02890 326803

www.iforgiveyoudaddy.co.uk A website to find somewhere to reach in a crisis or just to stop off and say hello.

www.matterstome.org Have an excellent DVD to educate our children about keeping safe and covers grooming and bullying, as well as the dangers of the internet with its chat rooms and webcams.

www.wrc-info.org
Watford Rape Crisis & Sexual Abuse Helpline
01923 249 511
0845 3011165

Opening Times
Mondays & Saturdays 10 am–12 noon
Wednesdays 7pm–9.30pm
Answerphone at other times

www.freefromaddiction.co.uk A website aimed at providing a peer to peer support service which helps to promote well-being and recovery in a safe non-judgmental environment for anyone wanting help with alcohol addiction.

www.survivorsmanchester.org.uk Supporting Male Survivors

www.holysouldier.ning.com Fighters against Child Abuse

www.ccpas.co.uk Churches Child Protection Advisory Service

CCPAS is an independent professional Christian based safeguarding charity that offers resources, training, advice and support in all areas of child protection and for adult survivors of childhood abuse. We engage with groups and individuals of many different faith backgrounds but also those with no religious affiliation. We advise local safeguarding Children Boards, Children's Services Departments, Adult Social Services, Police and other agencies across the UK.
As well as operating a 24 hour helpline, CCPAS has a number of resources for survivors of abuse, including books, leaflets and DVDs. All are available on the CCPAS website.

CCPAS, PO Box 133, Swanley, Kent, BR8 7UQ
Tel: 0845 120 45 50
Email: info@ccpas.co.uk

www.mosac.org.uk

Mosac is a voluntary organisation supporting all non-abusing parents and carers whose children have been sexually abused. We provide various types of support services and information for parents, carers and professionals dealing with child sexual abuse.
National Helpline: 0800 980 1958

HER Centre Ltd – The Forum @ Greenwich, Trafalgar Road, Greenwich, London, SE10 9EG. Telephone 0208 858 0748
Provides advice, information and support services to women who live, work or study in the borough of Greenwich.

www.supportline.org.uk We provide emotional support and information to all survivors of childhood abuse.

www.freewebs.com/sashpen Survivors of Abuse and Self-Harm. Email: sashpen@aol.com

S.A.S.H. is a pen friend network which understands and supports adult survivors (18+) of abuse and self-harming. S.A.S.H. aims to help and support survivors of abuse and self-harming by communicating in writing. We have a half yearly newsletter in which survivors can also voice their views, feelings and thoughts without being judged. S.A.S.H. is now free to join, but we have a small fee of £5.00 (or donation) for our newsletter: this is to cover postage and administration costs.

SPELTHORNE OPEN SPACE:
C/O 7 Falcon Drive, Stanwell, Staines, TW19 7EU
Telephone: 01784210661

One to one mutual support by survivors, for survivors, of childhood sexual abuse. Support via telephone or face to face. Open Mon.–Fri. 10 am–10 pm; Sat.–Sun. 10 am–4 pm. Also support for partners.

www.kidscape.org.uk Kidscape is committed to keeping children safe from abuse. Kidscape is the first charity in the UK established specifically to prevent bullying and child sexual abuse. Kidscape believes that protecting children from harm is key.

www.survivorsintransition.co.uk Childhood sexual abuse affects relationships, parenting and general well-being, in one in four women. SiT is a voluntary run drop-in centre for women who have experienced any form of childhood sexual abuse. The centre is a safe and welcoming place for all attending, so come along, meet other survivors, get some tips or advice on a range of issues or just have a cuppa and a chat.

www.pienmashfilms.com Pie 'n' Mash Films presents a collection of gritty thought-provoking British independent films and cutting-edge documentaries.

www.respond.org.uk Respond works with children and adults with learning disabilities who have experienced abuse or trauma, as well as those who have abused others, through psychotherapy, advocacy, campaigning and other support. Respond also aims to prevent abuse by providing training, consultancy and research.

www.aurorahealthfoundation.org.uk Specialist Therapy Centre for adult survivors of abuse and their supporters.

www.ffkfightingforkids.weebly.com Child abuse offends the basic values of our society. We have a responsibility to stand up and fight for the children.

www.lifecentre.uk.com Supporting survivors of rape and sexual abuse…**Unlocking the Past, Surviving the Present, Reclaiming the Future.** LifeCentre is a registered charity (Reg. charity No. 1127779) serving West Sussex. It offers face to face counselling for all victims of rape or sexual abuse, whatever their age, gender, ethnicity or religious beliefs. They have counsellors who specialise in working with under 18's, as well as with adults. Whilst the face to face counselling is in a specific geographical area, the helplines are available nationwide. The helplines are manned from 7.30 pm–10 pm on Sunday, Monday, Tuesday and Thursday evenings. Emails will be answered within 1 to 4 days of receiving it; text messages will be answered within 48 hours.

Kate Swift

Adult Helpline – 0844 8477879
Under 18's Helpline – 0808 8020808
Text line – 07717 989022
Email address – help@lifecentre.uk.com

www.alixchapel.co.uk Alix Chapel is the partner of
a survivor of childhood sexual abuse. Together Alix
and her partner are raising awareness.

Further sources of help and information:

Based Overseas:

www.whitedovesnest.com A website dedicated to
survivors of sexual abuse and those who support
them.

www.survivingspirit.com 'The mission of the
Surviving Spirit is to promote hope, healing and
help for those impacted by trauma, abuse or mental
health concerns through the use of the creative
arts.'

www.mskinnermusic.com An inspirational survivor,
song writer and speaker

www.unveilingthestigma.com 'Unveiling the Stigma'
is passionate about helping those who suffer with
Depression and Mental Illness. In view of this, we
have gathered the best resources on the web to
assist in your search. Whether you are suffering,
know of someone who is suffering, or simply wish

to gain knowledge...this website will help guide you in the right direction. We've done the research, so you don't have to.

www.johnmarkclubb.com 'Abuse does not have to be a life sentence.' John Mark Clubb

http://laurieannsmith.webs.com Protecting our children.

http://www.blogtalkradio.com/laurie-smith A survivor radio show with many interesting and helpful topics.

http://www.dreamcatchersforabusedchildren.com

www.womenspeakoutnow.com (Wo) Men Speak Out™ is a non-profit organization dedicated to eradicating rape, sexual assault and gender violence. We seek to educate both men and women, cultivating healthy relationships and gender equity.

www.unravelingabuse.com Unravelling the Threads: working through the Aftermath of Childhood Sexual Abuse is a memoir that offers understanding, hope, and concrete help for healing. (Christian Content)

www.saveaaron.com Aaron is a victim of sexual and psychological abuse. This page is for his cause and is managed by his sister, Mindy. Our mission is to bring Aaron home, empower victims, and raise awareness.

www.betrayedboys.com This site is primarily for male survivors of childhood sexual abuse, but we welcome all to join us in our journey to recovery. Sexual abuse does not just affect the victim – it affects all those who surround him, his partner, children, parents, brothers, sisters, and even friends – and we welcome those people also so they may find some help and advice on how to support the survivor in their family.

www.childabusemonument.com Healing, validation and inspiration are found at the Child Abuse Survivor Monument website.

SURVIVOR BLOGS...

http://jlreece.blog.com/ This blog shares my journey as a 25-year survivor of childhood sexual, physical, and emotional abuse, the lessons I've learned along the way, and the thoughts I have on how the events of the past continue to influence my day-to-day life.

http://itellmytruth.blogspot.com I tell my truth of surviving and thriving after childhood sexual abuse.

http://redawakening.com A brilliant blog by Mary Grimes

Recommended Books:

The Warrior Within ~ Christiane Sanderson
A One in Four handbook to aid recovery from
Childhood sexual abuse and violence.

I Forgive You Daddy ~ Lizzie McGlynn
A survivor's story

Whispers From Within ~ John Harrison
A survivor's poetry & writings

Stolen Innocence ~ Erin Merryn
A survivor's story

Living For Today ~ Erin Merryn

Silent No More ~ R.S.O.S.A/Kate Swift

Whispers of Hope ~ Kazzie Kennedy
(Available from www.kazziekbooks.com)

Hurt ~ Julie Webb-Harvey
(Available from www.liveitpublishing.com)

Boys Cry Too ~ John Mark Clubb
A survivor's story

A Life of Death: the Redemption ~ Laurie Ann
Smith

Diamonds from Coal ~ Clare White
A survivor's story

Kate Swift

The Throwaway Boy ~ Alix Chapel

'And Sew It Begins' ~ Debbie Roxborough
A survivor's story

The Echoes of My Mind & the Voices of My Soul ~
RS Redner
A series of poems that fall like footsteps through
the journey of life, from the peaks of love, through
to the dark valleys of depression

This Tangled Web ~ Kate Swift